PRAISE FOR
FLIPPING ADHD ON ITS HEAD

"Whether you are a mom, or a dad, or a teacher, or just somebody interested in learning about this fascinating condition, Dr. Jim is your man."

—EDWARD HALLOWELL, MD, coauthor of *Driven to Distraction*

"In tennis, there is nothing more critical than understanding, developing, and applying one's strengths toward success. If I were to take everything I know about coaching youth and apply it to parenting an ADHD child, this book would be it. High praise to Dr. Jim for *Flipping ADHD on Its Head*."

—CHUCK KRIESE, ACC's winningest tennis coach,
former US national coach

"Having combatted the devastating stigma and difficult challenges of mental health for over 30 years within my own family, I could not be more thrilled to see Dr. Jim finally getting this message out to the world. *Flipping ADHD on Its Head* is a welcome addition to the cause and the first book I'd recommend to any parent struggling with an ADHD child. Dr. Jim's approach gives so much hope to an area that has often been hopeless. Bless you, Dr. Jim, for this gift to the world."

—VAN EURE, International Restaurateur of the Year,
Chair, Walk for Hope

"I've read several books by physicians and clinicians about ADHD for patients and families—this is at the top of my list."

—MARK SIMMS, MD, Director of Children's Hospital in Milwaukee

"Dr. Jim has figured out a way to take what many doctors and people consider a handicap and turn it into an asset! This book will be life-changing for families all over our country!"

—BARRY FOOTE, Entrepreneur, former MLB Player and Coach

"This informative book provides awareness and understanding along with skills and strategies for parents of ADHD children . . . The specific strategies and concrete suggestions for helping ADHD children become successful learners, along with Dr. Jim's encouragement and positivity, result in a valuable resource for parents."

—DIANE PAYNE, principal, educator, author

FLIPPING
ADHD
ON ITS
HEAD

FLIPPING
ADHD
ON ITS
HEAD

How to Turn Your Child's "Disability"
into Their Greatest Strength

JIM POOLE, MD, FAAP

GREENLEAF
BOOK GROUP PRESS

Published by Greenleaf Book Group Press
Austin, Texas
www.gbgpress.com

Distributed by Greenleaf Book Group

For ordering information or special discounts for bulk purchases, please contact Greenleaf Book Group at PO Box 91869, Austin, TX 78709, 512.891.6100.

Design and composition by Greenleaf Book Group and Sheila Parr
Cover design by Greenleaf Book Group and Sheila Parr
Cover image © iStockphoto / ivanastar
Illustrations by Josh Malchuk

Publisher's Cataloging-in-Publication data is available.

Print ISBN: 978-1-62634-659-8

eBook ISBN: 978-1-62634-660-4

Part of the Tree Neutral® program, which offsets the number of trees consumed in the production and printing of this book by taking proactive steps, such as planting trees in direct proportion to the number of trees used: www.treeneutral.com

TreeNeutral

Printed in the United States of America on acid-free paper

19 20 21 22 23 24   10 9 8 7 6 5 4 3 2 1

First Edition

To all the children and adults with ADHD who have not yet experienced the joy, gift, and success of being FastBraiin

CONTENTS

FOREWORD

When you get to be my age, I'll be 70 by the time this book hits the market, well, you don't need to mess around anymore. You can pretty much tell when a person is good and when a person isn't inclined toward goodness. You can pretty much tell when someone has something interesting to say and when a person is just going to talk, which is not, in and of itself, a bad thing. After all, each person has to do something and if talking is what that person chooses to do, then so be it. It's just that it's my choice to listen, or not. And you can pretty much tell when someone is onto something and when someone isn't.

Dr. Jim Poole is onto something. What I especially like about what he's onto is that, unlike a new recipe for hummus, or a new route from D.C. to Philly, or a new take on the influence of soybeans in the history of Mississippi, what he's onto really matters—to me and to millions of children, parents, teachers, and anyone else who cares about kids and how they are educated and brought up these days.

You see, one of the most misunderstood, hotly debated, kicked around, and generally mangled topics in education, parenting, pediatrics, psychiatry, mental health, and child development is the subject Dr.

Jim is onto. It's the condition called ADHD, or attention deficit hyperactivity disorder—a misnomer and a mouthful of syllables if there ever was one. More people understand Martian weather forecasting than those who truly understand ADHD, but Dr. Jim is one of them.

There's no deficit of attention in ADHD, instead, there's an abundance. Hyperactivity is often not present at all. And, far from being a disorder, it can be a huge asset, as it is for David Neeleman, the man who founded JetBlue Airlines. But, you must beware because it can be a terrible disorder, as it is for the many people in prison who have it and the addicts and the unemployed who have it. This is why it is so important that we understand it and deal with it properly, so the kids who have it can grow up and become like David Neeleman, instead of being unemployed, in jail or addicted.

Dr. Jim is onto all of this. He wants to teach everybody about this condition that is so misleadingly called ADHD, help everybody so they can turn it into the asset it ought to be, and avoid the terrible outcomes that can result if it is not dealt with properly.

There's another thing I like as I get near 70. I like people who want to do good in this world. Don't you agree? I'm so fed up and just plain sick and tired of people who only want to make noise and get on the news and kick up a ruckus, not caring a hoot about the world as it continues to burst with sin and suffering. That phrase comes from my old friend Samuel Johnson. He lived a long time ago in the 18th century. But the world today still bursts with sin and suffering, and Dr. Jim is one of those people who actually wants to spend the time he has left doing something about it.

And the thing he knows enough about to do something is this condition so wrongly called ADHD. Dr. Jim will teach you what it ought to be called in this book. He coined a neat little term for it that I'll let him tell you. He will teach you how to turn the condition into an advantage for your child. He will also give you practical tools.

You see, he is a doctor, an old-fashioned, hands-on doctor. He listens. He laughs. He's a real person. He's lived long enough to be wise. And he's practical. That's the thing about busy pediatricians—they have to be practical. Otherwise, they get way backed up, and all the moms get mad at them, and no one wants a waiting room full of moms mad at them.

Whether you are a mom, or a dad, or a teacher, or just somebody interested in learning about this fascinating condition, Dr. Jim—who's onto something—is your man. Enjoy!

Edward Hallowell, MD
August 25, 2019

ACKNOWLEDGMENTS

In writing my first book, the list of those to thank includes nearly every-one I have known throughout my life. The most influential person along my journey was my father, Dr. Frank, who taught me that I can do anything I put my mind to, and who gave me the opportunity to try. His love for patients and his confidence in their ability to become successful regardless of their socioeconomic status had a resounding effect on me. My mother played a significant role in shaping my beliefs. Her unwavering positive spirit taught me the value of love and the importance of always "being there" for others. She encouraged me to write this book just before she passed away.

The friendships and those who have accepted and encouraged me are many, going back to my high school friends and my Clemson DKA fraternity brothers (Don A., Marion S., Bob S., Larry W., Sam C., Jim B., and Greg D.) who remain close to this day. Professionally, cardiologist Arno Hohn, MD, was my mentor and guided my training, and Dick Heath, MD, lieutenant colonel in my pediatric Army training, constantly pushed me to perfection in caring for my patients. Fred Burroughs, MD, one of the first African American pediatricians in NC, joined my practice late in his career, and was a trusted mentor until his recent passing.

Dr. Fred and my father constantly taught by their example how to care for patients physically, mentally, emotionally and spiritually. Rob Jeffers, MD, and I spent over 20 years together in pediatric residency, time in the Army, and private practice. Mandy Johnson and Joanne Wagner are medical colleagues who have been by my side for over 15 years. Our many discussions about medicine and life, as well as their encouragement and support, have meant a great deal to me. I'm also grateful for our unheralded staff, who help all those who come to our office in need of care, assistance, and support.

Barry Foote, a former MLB star and coach, has been instrumental in pushing me to take FastBraiin out into the world, and his support and guidance continue every day. David Katz, DO, has helped me have a greater understanding of functional medicine; Beth Briere, MD, in meeting the child "where they are"; Nicole Hanly, MEd, with the educational component of FastBraiin; and collegiate tennis coach Chuck Kriese and tennis professional Cliff Skakle with the brain and sports.

My family has continued to be supportive of FastBraiin since we started, persevering through 40 years of a busy pediatric practice, lively discussions, and multiple directions of a FastBraiin father and husband. Two of our sons, Jimmy and Christopher, both FastBraiin and former collegiate athletes at Clemson University, have endured the "learning curve" of understanding their father and are strong encouragers of the FastBraiin approach. This book would not be possible without our other son, Matthew, who sat in conversation with me for months after my heart surgery and helped give FastBraiin its direction. He has been instrumental in developing all aspects of this book, including researching, writing, and editing.

My wife, Lillian, is a constant and wonderful source of encouragement to me, our marriage, and FastBraiin. Especially meaningful to me has been her unfailing belief in God. She has not only edited this book but edited my life, and I am deeply grateful for her.

The one person who is the daily supporter and fighter for those with

FastBraiin is my nurse, Sommay. For the past 11 years, in addition to her nursing responsibilities with each patient, Sommay has made endless prescription refills and answered thousands of parent phone calls, carefully listening and responding to their unique needs and issues. She supports and encourages me daily in my "calling" to help others, no matter the time of day, the situation, or the problem. Her hard work and caring heart have helped FastBraiin achieve its 92% success rate.

Finally, I wish to thank my patients who have taken the FastBraiin approach and developed their strengths, which has allowed them to see that they are "okay" and have a unique ability to adapt, respond, and succeed in life. They continue to teach me the value of life and demonstrate how these strengths allow us to reach for the mountaintop and make a difference in the world.

INTRODUCTION

I can understand why you picked up this book. You are searching for an answer to the struggles that you, or someone you know, are having with an ADHD child. You may even struggle with ADHD yourself. I want to assure you—there is hope and a pathway to success.

There's nothing quite like the anxiety that we as parents experience over the future of our children—we are concerned about their health, their friends, their educations, their jobs, their marriages, their families, and ultimately, their happiness and success in the world. Trust me—I've been there, and sometimes I'm *still* there. I tell patients that I was a great pediatrician until I had kids! Each of our three boys is entirely different. The oldest is 110% ADHD, the second analytical and creative, and the third is ADHD with some obsessive-compulsive tendencies. I've learned a lot in 40 years of pediatrics, but that doesn't come close to the education I've received from the challenging task of parenting. Trying to figure out three different approaches to learning, discipline, and love for our boys was difficult. I am sure you know what I'm talking about. Parenting can be hard, complicated, and overwhelming, especially if you have an ADHD child!

So how do we go about unraveling the tangled subject of parenting and putting the ADHD child on a path to success? Do you remember the children's story "The Tortoise and the Hare"?

The moral of the story usually goes something like this: "Slow and steady wins the race." That's true, but there's a fundamental problem—the story addresses two very different animals with two very different natures. Yes, the slow and steady Tortoise won the race, but if the Hare had received a little coaching and not fallen asleep, he would have easily won. On another note, did he really lose? Or in losing, was he given the opportunity to learn from his mistakes so that he could win future races?

Who would you bet on in the second race?

In all my years of caring for patients, I've learned that ADHD children and adults are like hares, not tortoises. I often ask, "Why are we forcing these children and adults to think and act like the slow and steady Tortoise when everything in their nature says to be fast and adaptive like the Hare?" The ADHD individual shines in environments that demand speed, adaptation, and creativity. They don't do very well in slow-paced, analytical environments.

So, is ADHD about abnormalities or is it about differences? PC and Mac computers work differently. Is one abnormal? Of course not. They both shine in their own unique way. My passion for caring for ADHD children and adults, combined with a growing desire to affirm and utilize their strengths, has culminated in the development of the FastBraiin model. Our FastBraiin clinics have helped more than 7,000 children and adults achieve success in ways previously thought unreachable. Ninety-two percent of students involved in our FastBraiin program have improved their grades from C's, D's, and F's to making the A/B honor roll, and adults have found breakthroughs in time management, organization, and productivity. Many families report that overall relationships have deepened and that they no longer feel like life is out of control.

I'm not ashamed to tell you that I've struggled with ADHD my whole life—school was hard for me. I had significant trouble completing tasks, I was impulsive, and I wouldn't think about how my actions might affect others.

I still have ADHD. I always will, but now I see it as FastBraiin— as my strength.

Many years ago, I was at a medical meeting about ADHD children and adults. The facilitator was discussing brain scans showing abnormalities in ADHD brains. I raised my hand and with a smile asked, "I made it through medical school, and I now have a successful private practice. Are you telling me that I have abnormalities in my brain? Are you asking me to tell my patients that they are abnormal too?" The room was silent.

The purpose of writing this book is to give you a hope-filled perspective on ADHD and to help you and your ADHD child experience a life of happiness and success. I hope you will read with an open mind, letting go of the way you currently see ADHD. In the end, maybe you will understand why one of my 10-year-old patients remarked, "Mom, I feel sorry for those who aren't FastBraiin!"

Enjoy the journey!

I am Dr. Jim Poole, and I am FASTBRAIIN!

CHAPTER 1

A BROKEN SYSTEM

Why We Need to Flip
Our Approach

"There must be something wrong with me."

I wish I could say it was uncommon for me to hear the words "There must be something wrong with me," but the truth is, I hear similar statements like this every day in my office. On one occasion, I was seeing a lovely young lady (I'll call her Emily) for a routine physical. Her mom accompanied her, and the office visit quickly turned into a discussion about Emily's inability to sustain attention, focus, and do well in school. Emily's mom shared at length about her daughter's anxieties, struggles, and failures. Almost as an after-thought, she mentioned that Emily was an eighth-grade cheerleader, a social butterfly, and well liked by everyone, including her teachers. But here she was, sitting in a medical exam room, listening to her mother expound on all of her problems. The negatives unquestionably overshadowed her positives.

It's always difficult for me to hear about the failures, tears, and trials families experience when struggling with an ADHD child. Emily's mom was worried and concerned, and as usually happens in the first meeting, she began venting about all that Emily was doing wrong. I knew I needed to hear her out, but I also knew that listening compounded her daughter's pain, frustration, and sense of shame.

During their visit, I included the usual surveys and discussion points about ADHD, which included the suggestion that medication might improve her success at school. At the end of the visit, as I stood to escort Emily and her mother from the room, I saw tears in Emily's eyes. I knew she wanted to tell me something, so I asked her mom for a moment of privacy.

"Why are you crying?" I asked.

Through her tears, she responded, "There must be something wrong with me. You are giving me a pill!"

My heart sank. I paused and took a moment to reflect. How could this wonderful girl think there was something wrong with her?

Sure, she had trouble focusing and doing well in school, but we had also just talked about her incredible ability as a cheerleader, how she was a favorite among teachers and friends, and how she could think quickly and adapt instinctively to various situations. It was the ADHD discussion—being labeled with a disability and having to take a pill every day to focus and learn—that had upset her. Her eyes weren't bright with hope; they were filled with tears of shame and failure.

"What a huge disconnect," I thought. Emily's mother was also upset over the prospect of her daughter needing to take medication in order to be "normal" and to improve her grades.

I continued talking with Emily, focusing on her positives, when I had an "aha" moment.

"Emily, you are different," I said. "Your brain works fast, and that's what makes you a star. We will come up with a game plan to help you focus and reach your goals, but I want you to know that your difference is your strength."

While I talked further with both Emily and her mother, they began to understand the advantages of how her brain is wired, and I saw Emily's worry and concern start to shift. We discussed the role of medication and how it would help her brain, not change it—taking a pill was about allowing her true self to shine, just as running shoes help you run but don't make you a better runner.

Emily and her mother walked out of my office smiling, with a new, positive understanding of who she was and who she could become. Like so many others, Emily had been consumed with her anxieties and failures and couldn't see her great potential for success.

From ADHD to FastBraiin

"Something is wrong with me" is the constant refrain in the minds of countless children diagnosed with ADHD. The stigma is real, and it leaves a wake of devastation in its path. Its destructive power comes from the fact that the stigma reaches down into the child's core identity, shaping, influencing, and impacting everything that the child thinks and does. The transformation that I witnessed with Emily caused me to wonder if there might be a different approach. Looking into the eyes and hearts of so many parents and children with ADHD, I knew there had to be!

A few days after Emily's office visit, I had the opportunity to meet with several doctors and nurse practitioners from the area and shared my desire to change the negative stigma of ADHD.

One doctor responded, "Now that idea's out of the box."

Then another chimed in, "Dr. Jim doesn't have a box!"

At 1:00 a.m. the next morning, my mind was racing. I thought: "There has to be another approach to ADHD that doesn't focus on the negatives. Is ADHD *really* a disorder? What if ADHD is more about *how the brain thinks and learns*? What if having a fast brain is a great thing? These kids have fast brains. They don't have a disorder, they just need to control their impulsivity and attention. I don't have a disorder; my brain just works fast."

Then it hit me. "Fast Brain!"

I jumped out of bed, and in rushing to purchase a trademark for the name, I misspelled the word "brain." I added an extra "i," and the movement to flip ADHD on its head was born. **FASTBRAIIN!**

A BRIEF HISTORY OF THE LABEL

If you are like most parents, the current system of ADHD care has probably left you wondering if help is possible. Your child still struggles. You still struggle. You still have anxiety over your child's ability to achieve in school, maintain healthy peer relationships, and, most importantly, lead a happy, productive, and fulfilling life. You often feel hopeless because no one seems to understand you or your child. Although the current system has failed you, there is a path forward.

But if we are going to reinvent our approach, we must understand how and why the current method exists. Let's start at the beginning. The idea of ADHD was first mentioned in 1902 when a British pediatrician, Sir George Still, described the ADHD behaviors he saw as "an abnormal defect of moral control in children." Although Dr. Still found they couldn't sit still like other children, he interestingly affirmed they had the same level of intelligence.

WHAT IF ADHD IS MORE ABOUT HOW THE BRAIN THINKS AND LEARNS?

He used the word "hyper" to describe these kids, and "hyper" soon became synonymous with the condition itself. This "hyper" tendency became more and more apparent during the Industrial Revolution in the United States. Boys were customarily sent to factories to work on repetitive assembly lines, which are environments particularly frustrating to ADHD individuals (much like our present-day classrooms). The active ones could easily be singled out for not focusing, not staying on task, and moving around too much. In the 1960s, another name was chosen to label these children: Minimal Brain Dysfunction.

From *moral defect* to *brain dysfunction*—ADHD was certainly not off to a promising start. However, the move from morality to biology significantly reduced moral shame and placed us on a path toward understanding ADHD in terms of personal and genetic wiring.[1]

I still remember getting the original booklet describing children with attention issues and the apparent fact that they were "not normal." We were told to view these children as having a brain dysfunction. At the time, the medical community had no justification for it. Because they couldn't understand these "hyper" kids, they came up with Minimal Brain Dysfunction (MBD) as a way to label them. Imagine how receiving the MBD diagnosis must have felt to the child and parents. Imagine the emotional devastation.

Medical science, however, slowly began to shift its understanding of hyperactivity. Scientists pursued the theory that the problem had less to do with a physical abnormality and more to do with centers of the brain that were deficient in controlling attention and impulses. It was then that the label *Attention-Deficit/Hyperactivity Disorder* replaced Minimal Brain Dysfunction.

ADHD, therefore, appeared in the 1968 edition of the *Diagnostic and Statistical Manual of Mental Disorders* (the standard manual describing all recognized mental disorders as well as causes, risk factors, and treatments for each condition). In the 1980s, the *DSM* began recognizing and subdividing "hyper" behavior into two categories—internal only or internal and external. The medical community believed that hyperactivity was primarily an internal reality, which may or may not be accompanied by an external manifestation. One group was observed to be considerably better at controlling these external indications; however, they still had brains that were going fast!

Distinguishing between these two types of "hyper" led to the difference that we see today in ADHD and ADD. The "hyper" term was used to delineate the externally "hyper" individual (ADHD), and the term was dropped for the individual with a greater ability to control external movements (ADD). In this book, we will use ADHD and ADD synonymously, with the only difference being in external movement.

Later in the 1990s, there was an extensive study undertaken that examined pre- and post-diagnoses of thousands of kids, which sought to learn the common denominator of ADHD. During the study (and it is the best of its kind related to ADHD, occurring over 14 months with a two-year follow-up period), researchers determined that doctors must diagnose symptoms of ADHD before age seven and that an individual had to have a certain number of characteristics for the diagnosis to be made.

It wasn't long before the medical establishment changed its mind again and told providers they were "allowed" to make the medical diagnosis after observing fewer symptoms. Such a change in criteria led to a massive increase in the number of children and adults diagnosed with ADHD.

Certainly we saw this as a step of progress in our understanding of ADHD, as individuals who had previously suffered from ADHD in isolation and confusion began receiving proper care and attention. But even though this was another significant breakthrough, there remained much more to be done.

CURRENT UNDERSTANDING OF ADHD

The current *DSM* 5th edition (2013) treats ADD and ADHD similarly as a mental disorder. The manual asserts, "The essential feature of Attention-Deficit/Hyperactivity Disorder (ADHD) is a persistent pattern of inattention and/or hyperactivity-impulsivity that interferes with functioning or development."[2]

The medical community continues to break down the ADHD diagnosis into two primary forms, hyperactive (ADHD) and inattentive (ADD) types, with specific clarifiers for each.

NOTHING IS BEING DONE TO IDENTIFY AND PROMOTE THE STRENGTHS OF ADHD CHILDREN.

The hyperactive child (ADHD) often cannot sit still or stay seated, fidgets, talks a lot, interrupts others, cannot wait for his/her turn, and has trouble following behavioral norms. They display significant impulsivity with an inability to think through consequences or delay gratification.

The inattentive child (ADD) often makes careless mistakes, does not listen well, cannot sustain attention, is easily distracted, has trouble following directions, has trouble staying organized, has difficulty finishing tasks, and can be forgetful.

It's common for children to display symptoms characteristic of both types. Therefore, the *DSM* also describes a third option, the combined type.

For an official diagnosis, ADHD symptoms must also be evident in a variety of domains—across school, home, and social spheres. For example, if a child can't sit still at school but can sit still at home, there may be something else affecting the child. When professionals can detect these symptoms across domains, they make the mental disorder diagnosis of ADD or ADHD. The medical community currently affirms ADHD as a mental disorder affecting people of all ages, and it includes a widening range of symptoms.

On the one hand, it's good that we are closer to understanding the true nature of ADHD and that more people are receiving treatment, but on the other hand, there continues to be a massive disconnect. The current establishment puts Band-Aids on kids without healing anything at a deep level. Doctors diagnose children, but they leave them with a crushed sense of self, no direction in life, and a loss of hope for the future. As we saw in Emily's situation, it's not adequate care when a talented young individual like her breaks down in tears and remarks, "Something is wrong with me."

We've been zeroing in on the nuances of symptoms, but nothing has been done to identify and promote the strengths of ADHD children. In the decades since ADHD became a diagnosis, care for the ADHD individual has made very little progress.

IT'S TIME FOR A NEW APPROACH

Although it has taken roughly a century for the medical establishment to decide on the diagnosis of ADHD, they've hardly scratched the surface regarding how to properly treat and care for those with ADHD. You probably know this experientially, but it is worth drawing your attention to some alarming statistics.

The well-documented consequences of ADHD as they pertain

to our current mental health crisis permeate the medical literature. We now see ADHD as a lifelong issue that can (1) alter emotional centers within the brain, (2) cause a great deal of personal and societal harm, and (3) overlap and influence other mental health conditions. Professionals sometimes link ADHD with clinical depression, anxiety, obsessive-compulsive disorder, tic disorders, and bipolar disorder, each of which may significantly reduce self-esteem, school and work performance, and social well-being.

The delay between the onset of symptoms and any form of decisive intervention can be as long as 10 years, spanning the most critical period of mental development for children and adolescents. The onset of ADHD in youth, when combined with a lack of proper care, can lead to suicide, violence, and major mood disorders. The delay results in the "side effect" of poor self-esteem and a lost sense of one's place within their peer group. Poor grades in school and behavior difficulties may contribute to issues that plague the child for years.

> ## ADHD CHILDREN, BY THE TIME THEY ARE 12, MAY RECEIVE 20,000 MORE NEGATIVE MESSAGES THAN THEIR PEERS.

Dropout rates are linked heavily with ADHD, and a majority find themselves caught up in drugs and crime. A large percentage of those suffering from addictions also have ADHD. And the connection between addictions and ADHD is especially troubling given the current opioid crisis. In 2016, more than 64,000 people died of a drug overdose, which was an increase of over 20% more

than the previous year.[3] In 2018, physicians began to more frequently prescribe ADHD medications that carried a greater potential for abuse, such as amphetamines.

Additionally, the financial impact of ADHD for the country is
thought to be over 200 billion dollars a year.[4] This might sound like
an exaggeration, but it makes sense once you factor in all the medical costs for office visits, medications, and the loss of personal work
due to missed time taking a child to the office or because of a suspen-
sion from school. The number could be even higher if we include the
further impact of ADHD and its relationship to other mental health
conditions, tendencies toward addiction, and the financial burden of
the state through incarcerations and governmental assistance.

The most alarming perspective comes from a spread of longi-
tudinal data presented by Russell Barkley, PhD, one of the world's
leading ADHD professors. He showed tangible evidence that
ADHD children, when untreated, are 1.8 times more likely to die
in any 4-year period than the general population. This tragic likelihood then doubles as the child enters adulthood. And in the full
analysis, it means the average ADHD individual is likely to have
their life expectancy cut short by 13 years. For those with the worst
cases of ADHD, this means a reduction of 20–25 years when compared to the general population.[5] In light of these statistics and the
reality of ADHD, *the need for a new approach to diagnose and care
for ADHD children and adults cannot be overstated.*

CARE THAT CULTIVATES THE STIGMA

The diagnosis of Attention-Deficit/Hyperactivity Disorder (ADHD)
carries an overall negative connotation. Whatever you may believe
it to be, ADHD is not a neutral label. It's full of negativity, and this
negativity reaches down into the core of one's identity. Too often
children and adults end up believing, "I'm not okay. Something is

wrong with me. I'm not normal." It's easy to understand why when you realize ADHD children, by the time they are 12, may receive 20,000 more negative messages than their peers.[6]

Fig. 1.0

These negative patterns of thinking have grave consequences and, in many ways, become self-fulfilling prophecies, determining the trajectory of their lives. Recent studies indicate that around 11% of US children ages 4 through 17 have been diagnosed with ADHD, making it now the most common "mental health" disorder in children and adolescents, accounting for over 40% of all mental health cases.[7] That means 11% of our children live daily with a sense of shame, disappointment, and failure. And this cloud of negativity puts kids on a path of significant risk if they do not receive proper intervention and support.

I often ask parents, "Do you believe children with ADHD are really not okay? Is there really something wrong with your child?" I'm not saying that they don't have weaknesses and don't need to develop mechanisms of self-monitoring and control. I'm asking in a generalized sense, "Are they doomed to failure?"

If over 6.4 million children in the US have been diagnosed with ADHD, should we be calling ADHD a mental disorder? That's more than the population of left-handed individuals. At what point do enough people have ADHD that it becomes normal? The symptomatic range for an ADHD diagnosis continues to widen, with more and more children and adults diagnosed. At what point will we consider that we, as the medical establishment, may be doing something wrong? We've had blind spots in the past—we have to assume we have blind spots now.

Stephen Hinshaw, PhD, and Richard Scheffler, PhD, remind us in their book, *The ADHD Explosion*, that "the huge variation across people in terms of attention span, inhibitory control, and reward sensitivity is strongly related to genes, yet such differences were not terribly salient or impairing until society decided that all children needed to sit still in classrooms."[8] Has society decided the standard of testing for kids and determined, on an unfounded basis, that ADHD is an unquestionable impairment?

Fig. 1.1

Our standard of testing not only inaccurately assesses a child's true ability and potential but has tragic ramifications for the child and their future. Failure to succeed within the traditional education system cripples ADHD children's confidence and strips them of their imagination and passion for life.

Einstein once cautioned, "Everybody is a genius, but if you judge a fish by its ability to climb a tree, it will live its whole life believing that it is stupid." In the same way, our ADHD children are judged on their ability to climb the tree of traditional education, and when they fail to perform well, they believe the lie that they are stupid. Squeezing them into these predetermined boxes can then have a host of adverse outcomes.

I contend that the problem of ADHD has less to do with our impulsive children and more to do with the current negative diagnosis, care, and lack of understanding and appreciation for the ADHD brain. The ADHD brain learns very well, but not in the traditional confines of the classroom.

SUCCESS FOR ADHD INDIVIDUALS IS DETERMINED BY TWO ESSENTIAL VARIABLES: CONFIDENCE AND TRAINING.

It is true that some ADHD individuals have significant difficulties in life—there's no denying that. But others have become highly successful. I've seen many ADHD children become very successful artists, musicians, athletes, teachers, doctors, business people, sales people, venture capitalists, and CEOs (this may make you think twice about those early report cards with poor grades).

It's becoming increasingly common for celebrities to acknowledge their own journeys with ADHD. Athletes such as Michael Phelps, Cammi Granato, and Simone Biles; creative stars like

Justin Timberlake, Jim Carrey, and Will Smith; and entrepreneurs like David Neeleman, Sir Richard Branson, and Dean Kamen have all come forward embracing their ADHD, many claiming that ADHD is the difference maker in their success. Biographies also suggest that Leonardo da Vinci, Thomas Edison, Winston Churchill, and Walt Disney may have been individuals with ADHD. Thom Hartmann, in his book *The Edison Gene: ADHD and the Gift of the Hunter Child*, argues from an evolutionary perspective that those with ADHD were critical to the development and survival of the human race and are possibly the key to our future success as well.

What are we doing to our entrepreneurs and creative problem-solvers when we put them in a box early in life? Why do we want them to start thinking like everyone else when that's not how advancement and breakthroughs generally happen? I've always loved what Henry Ford once said: "If I had asked my customers what they wanted, they would have said a faster horse!" Fast-Braiin individuals are uniquely gifted with this kind of out-of-the-box thinking—they don't have boxes—and need to be set free to explore their unique patterns of thought.

ARRIVING AT FASTBRAIIN

For years I've been researching the brain, and specifically its relationship to those with ADHD. In my quest, I resolved to answer one question: Does the ADHD brain uniquely fit individuals for success?

I discovered something amazing—ADHD individuals have incredible strengths, and these advantages seem to be across the board. They are risk-takers, they are imaginative, they are creative, they think outside the box, they adapt quickly to changing environments, they are passionate, and they are personable—all incredible traits that give ADHD individuals the ability to thrive.

It became impossible for me to affirm the commonly held belief that children with ADHD have a mental disorder. About 11% of our population has ADHD (which is growing daily), and there's now a continuum of ADHD (it's becoming less clear who has it). Those who have ADHD have remarkable abilities—abilities that more often than not propel them forward rather than backward.

Disability is a label given within a specific context of testing, dependent upon the perspective from which one is looking. Dr. Edward Hallowell, a leading ADHD psychiatrist and foremost believer in the gift of ADHD, has pointed out that each of the three common traits of ADHD—impulsivity, distractibility, and hyperactivity—have a corresponding strength in a different environment. Impulsivity, when used correctly, corresponds with creativity. Distractibility showcases a high degree of curiosity. And hyperactivity is nothing more than energy. In certain contexts, who wouldn't desire creativity, curiosity, and energy? It all depends on your vantage point.[9]

CONTEXT IS EVERYTHING

NEGATIVE CONTEXT VS	POSITIVE CONTEXT
EASILY DISTRACTED	CURIOUS
FORGETFUL	ENGAGED IN THE MOMENT
CAN'T STAY ON POINT	SEES THINGS OTHERS MISS
HYPERACTIVE	ENERGETIC
IMPULSIVE	CREATIVE
DISORGANIZED	SPONTANEOUS
STUBBORN	PERSISTENT
INCONSISTENT	FLASHES OF BRILLIANCE

Fig. 1.2

Figure 1.2 summarizes the most common "negative" aspects of ADHD along with their positive counterparts.[10]

But another question needs to be answered: "If ADHD is a strength, why do some people with ADHD struggle to succeed?" Since talent's not in question, we believe success for ADHD individuals is determined by two essential variables—confidence and training. To illustrate, a tennis player who has confidence but does not have training will struggle. And a tennis player who has training but not confidence will also struggle. But a tennis player with confidence and training will find success. And so it is with the ADHD individual.

Therefore, I believe the current problem for ADHD children is twofold: (1) the diagnosis is negative, leaving children feeling defeated, and (2) the care is incomplete, leaving children without the proper skills needed to thrive. To put it in the affirmative, we need (1) a diagnosis that empowers ADHD children and their families and (2) a plan of care that effectively trains ADHD children to utilize their unique strengths for success.

For Emily, she was given a one-two punch of negativity when she was told, "You have Attention-Deficit/Hyperactivity Disorder" (a defeating diagnosis) and then given a pill intended to "fix" her (a defeating approach). She can't help but walk out of the office upset if that is the extent of the conversation. Her sense of defeat influences everything from her grades to her social life, and becomes the trajectory of her life.

Imagine if we instead said, "Your brain has strengths (empowering diagnosis), and moving forward, we are going to teach you about your brain and train you to optimize your unique strengths (empowering approach)."

What a difference this would make for your ADHD child! How empowered would your child feel, leaving that office visit? A positive and empowering model of care transforms lives, brightens faces, and offers hope to individuals and families.

Maybe that sounds too good to be true. Maybe you're wondering if that is even possible. Absolutely. We've seen it happen too many times to doubt it. With the right help, you and your child can get there!

SUMMARY

- Past and current approaches to ADHD are negative in diagnosis and care, failing children by leaving them discouraged, defeated, and without hope.
- The FastBraiin approach to ADHD is positive in its diagnosis and in its plan of care.
- The FastBraiin approach centers on recognizing and developing the strengths of ADHD individuals and seeks to empower them with the tools necessary to thrive.

CHAPTER 2

FLIPPING THE SYSTEM

Essential Components of Effective ADHD Care

*"The approach must be positive,
or it will fail, and the approach must
be comprehensive, or it will fail."*

In the previous chapter, I stated that a successful ADHD approach must empower children and effectively train them to utilize their unique strengths. In over 40 years of caring for ADHD individuals, I have found that to accomplish this we need an approach that is at its core positive (including the diagnosis and plan of care) and comprehensive (including every aspect of one's life).

Like two wings on a plane, both components are critical. The approach must be positive, or it will fail, and the approach must be comprehensive, or it will fail. We need both components for ADHD children and adults to fly successfully, and until we fix the system, the stigma of ADHD and ineffective care will continue to impair children and families.

Let's take a closer look at the two primary components of the FastBraiin approach to ADHD.

A POSITIVE APPROACH

I was a pretty good swimmer as a kid, so one year my coach bumped me up to the next age group. As you can imagine, this was a serious boost to my confidence. However, once the season started, I lost every race. Losing was not fun, and my chances of winning were going down, so what did I do? When the season was over, I quit and resolved never to try the sport again.

The reason is simple. Humans are emotional creatures, with emotions at the core of everything we do. Neuroscientists have proven there are over 1,000 connections in the brain that are hardwired to our emotional and reward centers, and it is these centers that drive our behavior, whether or not we are aware of it.

There is nothing like having the reward center in your brain activated with a dopamine surge, whether it's from making a three-pointer in basketball, having a warm donut with a cold glass of milk, beating the bad guys in a video game, or getting high on a drug. When the reward center lights up, we want more of whatever it is that gives us that "good feeling."

While I was winning at swimming, I wanted to keep practicing; I wanted to keep winning. I loved the feeling I had when I won races. Once I transitioned to the next age group and began losing, my reward center started pushing me in other directions. I had the choice of either becoming a better swimmer—which seemed impossible to me—or quitting and finding pleasure in a different activity. Perceiving no reward in swimming, quitting was the natural decision.

POSITIVE DIAGNOSIS = POSITIVE LABEL

Now, imagine that instead of feeling like a loser in sports, you feel like a loser in life. Imagine how that impacts you. You might get depressed, angry, anxious, frustrated, and inclined to act out. You might tragically even quit. And this is precisely what happens to our ADHD kids—they feel like losers at life.

Why do ADHD children of all ages feel like this? It's all they hear. A deep sense of negativity usually begins in elementary school and gets worse within seconds of receiving a diagnosis of ADHD. By definition, in their diagnosis they start hearing and identifying with the words deficit and disorder. Who wants that said to them? And who wants to take a pill the rest of their life as a "fix"?

Too often the message ADHD kids receive from doctors, parents, teachers, and friends is the same: "You are a problem. You don't measure up. You are a failure. You have a disability that prevents you from focusing and from controlling your thoughts and actions."

We may not say it in those exact words, but that's what kids perceive and internalize. And their perception colors their reality. The message bombards them from every angle, and at some point they start to believe it.

> **IF OUR CHILDREN'S GREATEST PREDICTOR OF SUCCESS IS THEIR PERCEPTION OF PERSONAL VALUE AND ABILITY, THEN OUR MESSAGE MUST CHANGE.**

Over time, this belief destroys their life. It's like telling the Little League kid going up to bat that he is going to strike out and never get on base. How is that child supposed to swing with any confidence? He can't. But this isn't how we treat our Little Leaguers, is it? No, we understand it's baseball and that children need our unconditional support, regardless of the outcome. Top hitters in Major League Baseball get out 66% of the time, and we consider them stars!

So why do we change our approach when it comes to ADHD? If our children's greatest predictor of success is their perception of personal value and ability, then our message must change. As it stands, ADHD kids, in general, believe they have little worth and can't perform, and their attitude, behavior, and grades bear this reality out. Any ADHD program, therefore, that is not positive at its core is a limited, failing program.

Dale Archer, MD, addressing our failing approach in his book *The ADHD Advantage,* laments, "I wish there was a better word for it than diagnosis or disorder because, except for the far end of the continuum, this is not an illness that needs to be treated."[11]

There *is* a better word for it—FastBraiin—built on assessing and developing strengths, not diagnosing disease. That's why the first thing we do in caring for ADHD individuals in our clinics is remove the negative label, Attention-Deficit/Hyperactivity Disorder, and replace it with the positive label, FastBraiin.

"When children first present with symptoms," says Dr. Archer, "why aren't we telling them that they are three times more likely to form their own business, will thrive in disruptive situations, will embrace adventure and are adept at multi-tasking, as opposed to giving them a diagnosis and a pill?" Telling a child they are FastBraiin is like telling a Little Leaguer they are an all-star. This fires up the reward center in the brain, engages the emotions, and allows the child to connect with life in a positive manner. The positive label then creates more confidence, more enjoyment, and more potential for success.

Fig. 2.0

FastBraiin individuals gain a new identity that serves to reinforce their potential positively. They begin believing they can perform well because they understand who they are. Their identity has shifted, and the ripple effect is without borders. Believing they are an all-star, with a gifted mind, capable of so much, they naturally step up to the plate and swing for the fence.

POSITIVE CARE

The core of the positive FastBraiin philosophy revolves around changing one's identity, but the positive approach must also permeate every realm of care. To continue with the Little League analogy, not only do we need to instill confidence by telling and showing the child that they can hit, we also need to do everything in our power to help the child relate to baseball positively—that is, to see baseball as beneficial, rewarding, and worth the effort.

Just because a child believes they are a great hitter doesn't necessarily mean they will want to play or be able to play. Just because a child believes they are smart intellectually doesn't mean they will put their intelligence to work.

To get there, we must build a bridge of positivity between the child and the child's activity. Until the child relates to what they're doing with a positive emotion, it will be tough to produce anything of lasting value.

> ## TELLING A CHILD THEY ARE FASTBRAIIN IS LIKE TELLING A LITTLE LEAGUER THEY ARE AN ALL-STAR.

When I didn't perceive any pleasure or positivity in swimming, I quit and got involved in another sport. It was a decision based on emotion, not ability. Unfortunately, the activity we're focusing on is not swimming, baseball, or video games (that would be easier) but school. Our great challenge is to create a bridge of positive emotion between the child and school—a tough battle, because our culture and most school systems have stripped excitement and pleasure from the classroom.

The excitement of a good grade has been replaced by the relief of not getting a bad grade, which is ultimately the relief of not getting into trouble at home. Just ask your child, "Are you more excited about getting a good grade or not getting into trouble for a bad grade?"

The need to pass quizzes and end-of-grade tests has replaced the excitement of the learning process and short-circuited personal passions. Of course benchmarks are necessary, but when benchmarks become the goal, they fail to motivate and inspire. Instead, we must invest in and tap into our children's passions, cultivating

a genuine love for learning, and connecting th
quizzes with the hope of one day becoming a
developer, doctor, business professional, or w
sions and strengths lead them to become.

School is doubly challenging for FastBraiin kids because they
have trouble perceiving long-term rewards at the end of the tun-
nel. ADHD experts Craig Surman, MD, and Tim Bilkey, MD, in
their insightful book *Fast Minds*, describe how the ADHD brain is
predisposed toward impulsivity, which they say ultimately is a failure to hold long-term rewards in view because of a stronger desire
for immediate gratification. And the further out the reward, the
harder it is for ADHD individuals to perceive it.[12] Therefore, we
should be especially mindful to connect ADHD children's present
circumstances with future possibilities. Can we honestly expect
kids to sit still in hard chairs for eight hours a day, doing what
seems to be irrelevant and boring and do so with good behavior?
Can we, as adults, stay focused like that at work?

WE MUST INVEST IN AND TAP
INTO OUR CHILDREN'S PASSIONS.

It's up to you as the parent to infuse as much of your child's
environment as possible with positive words and experiences. Every
time you speak with your child about grades, every time homework
comes up, every time you discuss a subject of study, you must find a
way to be positive. Dr. Hallowell believes that "more than anything
else, [ADHD] kids need someone to detect the beginnings of what's
positive in their oddball, offbeat, exasperating, or disruptive ways."[13]
That's what it's about—pointing out and affirming the positives.

Celebrating the positives requires an active search on your part. At first, you might not find anything positive, but with diligent effort, you can find it. This is the hard but rewarding work that you must do. Without it, your child will only pick up on your negativity. Notice how Hallowell points to "the beginnings" of what's positive. You want to celebrate the positive in your child, regardless of the degree of positivity. Any improvement is worth pointing out, no matter how small. In the beginning, choosing to be supportive might take some adjustment or personal reminders, but over time it will become a natural and joyful part of your relationship.

Being positive, however, does include having tough conversations. Your FastBraiin child looks to you as the parent, as the authority figure, and requires the boundaries and guidance you supply. But even in those times when discipline or correction needs to be implemented, you have to still frame everything in a positive light. And yes, this will take lots of patience and perseverance on your part. Remember, just as your child is a work in progress, the same is true for you!

I regularly hear from parents: "He will not pass his end-of-grade testing" or "She might be retained," rather than looking hard at the issues and how to take steps forward. Teachers use this tactic by encouraging you to see a physician for "behavior" medicine. This negativity gets passed on to the child. As parents, you need to become more positive, consistently looking for the good in any situation. You must highlight the path that leads to success.

Pointing out the positive will not only keep your child engaged but also create an emotional environment that increases the likelihood of learning and correction. Studies confirm that if kids are stressed, anxious, and perceive no emotional payoff in school, their brains will shut down. Negative emotions destroy a child's learning ability.

When we change to a positive approach and begin rewarding

small successes, regardless of the activity, we are giving small tokens of support for the effort. It's vital that you do not reward your child because of the action or grade but instead reward because of the effort. Consistent, positive affirmation and encouragement supports the reward center of the brain, which will naturally cause the child to strive for more, just like when they win a video game or get a base hit. I remember watching one of my patients, Stephanie, go from D's and F's to all C's. She was so excited. I praised her efforts and told her I wanted more! She couldn't believe that I was asking her to produce even better grades, nor did she at that moment feel it was within her ability to do so. But with positive reinforcement and a focus on continual effort, her next report card was filled with A's and B's!

A COMPREHENSIVE APPROACH

We've seen how being positive can translate into action steps that lead to success. This is just the start. We must also offer comprehensive care. Any good tennis player knows that they must focus on several key areas—grip, racquet speed, balance, footwork, strategy, mental game, physical conditioning, flexibility, and overall health.

What would happen to tennis players who spend all of their time in the weight room? Their chances of becoming great, or even an average player, are slim. There's a lot more to playing tennis than developing muscles.

And that's how we often view ADHD. We fail to consider its complexity and imagine there is a simple, single solution. Many may go the medicine-only route and try throwing a pill at the problem to "fix" their child. Medicine may be a piece to the puzzle—and it can be a valuable piece—but it's not everything. That would be like fixing only the tires on a car that's been totaled in a crash and thinking it was ready for the road.

For others, the solution for their child lies in talking to an educator, seeing a therapist, or making dietary changes. None of these categories in and of themselves can help the ADHD mind succeed. ADHD is far too complicated and multi-faceted, but most clinics tailor to patients in this simplistic manner. Physicians prescribe medicine and send their patients home without further guidance, and educators work with students on math problems but fail to address their anxiety. Professionals rarely work together or lean on each other's expertise in caring for ADHD individuals. It's no surprise then that parents usually end up doing the same thing.

Fig. 2.1

FastBraiin is different. We see the absolute need for ADHD care to be multifaceted. We offer a comprehensive and integrated approach that focuses on three main areas: medical, behavioral, and educational. We look at many categories within each domain, including nutrition, use of supplements, sleep, exercise, mindfulness, learning techniques, school strategies, parental involvement, psychological counseling, and use of medication.

> # MOST PEDIATRICIANS ARE LUCKY IF THEY SAW 10 ADHD PATIENTS DURING THEIR MEDICAL SCHOOL TRAINING.

Our FastBraiin approach centers on doing everything possible to help the child, and that means leveraging anything and everything we can to that end. It's not so much that we desire to be a one-stop shop as it is that we believe effective care demands a spectrum of modalities. One of our pediatricians, Beth Briere, MD, a nationally known ADHD pediatrician working with FastBraiin, sums up our FastBraiin philosophy like this: "We must meet the patients where they are, in their world, and in their universe!"

Why Did ADHD Treatment Become So Narrowly Focused?

The answer is simple, and we doctors are at least partially to blame for becoming narrow in our approach. It wasn't intentional; it's just how information has been passed down from one generation to the next. We were trained to treat disease rather than to care holistically for an individual. Western medicine was built on the principle of being able to isolate a problem and fix it. Only recently has the West looked more closely at how different organs and systems in the body are connected. Most professionals know very little about

ADHD and are therefore quick to prescribe a pill as the "fix." And what physician is going to spend a lot of time talking to a parent and child about their anxiety and difficulty in school?

Medical school didn't train us that way. Instead, what do most doctors do? They write a prescription and tell the patient to come back in two to four months, not spending time on the issues of concern but, instead, hoping for the best. Most pediatricians are lucky if they saw 10 ADHD patients during their medical school training, and that usually happened during a one-month rotation, with little focus on co-existing mental health conditions and virtually no opportunity for patient follow-up.

I also don't know of any medical university that teaches medical students or pediatric residents the issues that occur within the classroom and education system. We learn about poison control, ear infections, how to save a one-pound newborn, and the need for bicycle helmets, but we learn very little about mental health or education. Times have changed, and it is critical that our training change as well. One in five children will have a mental health issue of some kind, and 40% of those children will have ADHD.

LOOKING AT THE WHOLE PERSON

At our FastBraiin clinics, we first give children and adolescents a full physical examination, which includes checking their blood pressure, growth and development, coordination, vision, hearing, and lab values that particularly affect learning and attention, such as vitamin D, folate, B6, B12, and iron. We want to know a lot of the variables that might be contributing to an individual's ADHD, and this begins at the physical level. These variables underscore the many ways a problem can manifest as an attention issue, which is impossible to discern from a simple survey or computer test.

BETWEEN 50% AND 70% OF ADHD INDIVIDUALS HAVE CO-EXISTING CONDITIONS.

It's common for us to find deficiencies in vitamin D, high levels of lead, malfunctioning thyroids, and obstructive sleep apnea. Sometimes treatment of these issues results in the ADHD symptoms lessening or completely disappearing. We also need to rule out multiple conditions that may masquerade as ADHD. So our next step is to focus on the mental aspects of our patients. Depending upon the study, somewhere between 50% and 70% of those with ADHD have co-existing conditions, including anxiety, depression, bipolar disorder, learning disabilities, emotional dysregulation, oppositional defiant disorder, and obsessive-compulsive disorder. ADHD symptoms may overlap with, exacerbate, or be caused by these other issues. The following graph represents the data spread of one study examining 1,000 ADHD patients with co-existing conditions.

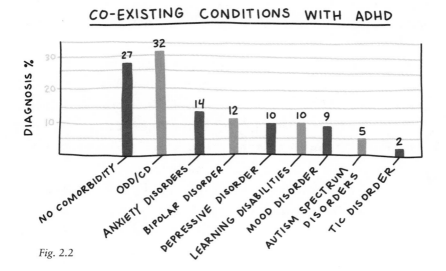

Fig. 2.2

We then begin the search for significant social or biological stresses that may be present, specific genetic factors, and relevant family history, including the possible impact that foster care or parental separation may have had on the patient. Until we discover the root causes of a patient's symptoms and have an understanding of the issues, progress will remain at a superficial level.

Consider a typical scenario of caring for a patient who exhibits the co-existing condition of depression. If the root issue of depression masks itself as ADHD, then methods of treating ADHD will not help the problem. The root issue of depression needs to be addressed as it relates to depression, not as ADHD.

I remember one patient I had, Katie, who was a college sophomore and struggling with studying and getting work done. Because she had been treated previously for ADHD with little benefit, she came in frustrated and didn't believe her situation could improve. After a careful analysis, we realized her focus and task-management difficulties stemmed from an underlying problem with anxiety. As we shifted the target away from ADHD and toward anxiety, her symptoms cleared up. She regained focus and attention and went on to graduate from college with an A average and is now a successful teacher and taking online graduate studies. What made the difference for Katie was our willingness to make the correct diagnosis and properly care for her.

Co-existing issues like depression may, however, play a more interactive role. In such cases, we must address both ADHD and depression. After a careful analysis of the multiple factors present, we develop an effective strategy to deal with both components from a medical, behavioral, and educational perspective.

Educationally, we focus on how the child learns. Figuring out the way each child processes and understands information is critical. We explore different methods of learning (visual, kinesthetic, or auditory) and seek to implement strategies that best fit the child.

We look at other factors that correlate with learning, such as their home environment, how and when they do homework, and the amount of screen time on the TV, computer, or phone.

> # WE CANNOT BE CONTENT TO PRESCRIBE A SINGLE SOLUTION TO SOLVE THE COMPLEXITY OF ADHD.

Helping students overcome homework and test anxiety is as important as learning how to study and focus. We train students to utilize study skills such as speed, repetition, music, and memory techniques to alleviate fear and anxiety.

It's well documented that exercise, recreation, play, and overall health have a critical role in learning. Once a child understands how to learn, their confidence grows, and the sky becomes the limit for what they can achieve. In this fashion, we provide complete and sufficient care to the patient, with long-lasting results.

PUTTING THE TEAM TOGETHER

FastBraiin brings together a team of professionals in different fields who understand ADHD from the same positive and comprehensive perspective. Our FastBraiin clinics include a trained provider (physician or nurse practitioner), a professional counselor, and an educator.

Does the child need to see a provider? Yes. Does the child need to see a counselor? Yes. Does the child need to see an educator? Yes. So why not put these professionals under one roof? Fig. 2.3 visually summarizes how we think through effective care at FastBraiin.

From a positive perspective, we form a comprehensive and individualized plan of care for each of our patients.

Until you find a team that will work with you, it's on you as the parent to act as the point person, coordinating care for your child across different modalities. Such a task, however, can be incredibly difficult and confusing to navigate.

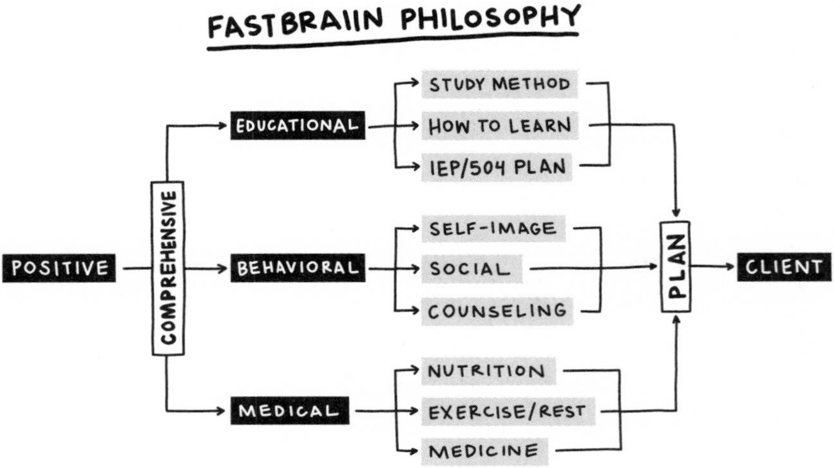

FASTBRAIIN PHILOSOPHY

Fig. 2.3

In fact, it often creates new challenges that parents aren't expecting. We frequently hear parents ask, "What if the professionals I visit are on different pages about how to help my child?" You may end up having an educator who offers different advice from a counselor, and both different from a doctor. How do you get all of these professionals working together from the same positive perspective and understanding of ADHD? It can be quite overwhelming to piece it all together.

If you are not near a FastBraiin clinic, that's okay. It will require a little more work, but it's doable. With some homework, and talking to your child's professionals, you can create a system that works. Begin by finding a provider you trust and who is knowledgeable about ADHD. If they see ADHD as a strength, all the better. Get your child involved with counseling to work on their anxiety, depression, or social skills. Have your child see an educator who understands the strengths and weaknesses of the ADHD individual and who can help your child develop according to their learning style. In addition to finding professionals with experience and knowledge, it's imperative to see professionals who will believe in your child and relate to them positively. Don't be fooled by credentials.

If they have the knowledge but don't work well with your child, you may experience counterproductive results. The relational connection is critical. We cannot be content to prescribe a single solution to solve the complexity of ADHD. Whether it's a pill, a tutoring program, or any other single solution, by itself it will fall far short in helping your child reach their potential. Instead, we need a system of care that addresses the whole child in their entire environment. Neither can we be satisfied with any protocol that is not positive at its foundation, because this may be the real difference maker. Once you can implement a plan that's positive and comprehensive, you will begin to see amazing results in your child's confidence and self-esteem at home, school, and in overall life success.

SUMMARY

- Effective ADHD care must be both positive and comprehensive.
- ADHD children are incredibly complex, and we must care for them in a personal and understanding way.
- The most crucial step in care is to change the ADHD child's identity from a negative to a positive self-image. Once their new identity is in place, building positive

connections between the child and their activities must continue. Cultivating a positive environment will help keep the child engaged and facilitate learning possibilities.

- ADHD care must include medical, behavioral, and educational components to address the full range of concerns with ADHD individuals.

CHAPTER 3

FLIPPING PARENTING

How to Become a Hero
for Your Child

*"Finding a path forward involves much
more than a doctor, a teacher, or anything a
computer program can offer—it involves you,
the parent—you are the most critical factor
in your child's success."*

Wikipedia defines a hero as "someone who, in the face of danger, combats adversity through impressive feats of ingenuity, bravery, or strength, often sacrificing his or her personal concerns for some greater good."[14] Combating adversity in the face of danger sounds a bit like parenting, doesn't it? And when you have an

ADHD child, the challenge of parenting intensifies. Every day is a battle. Some days there are wins, and some days there are losses—for you and your child.

Fighting for our kids is a tough task and not something for the faint of heart. To "win" the fight may take "feats of ingenuity, bravery, or strength," but don't let that scare you, because you have these qualities within you. The question is, "Are you in the fight? Are you in the trenches with your child? Or have you given up and checked out?" Being a hero does not mean being perfect—it means trying, admitting mistakes, asking for help when needed, and getting back up after getting knocked down.

It is easy to fall into the trap of avoiding responsibility for helping your child by outsourcing their issues to doctors, educators, or special computer programs, hoping your child can be "fixed." Outsourcing care would make life easier, but unfortunately, there is currently (in 2019) no test for ADHD and no known cure. Despite this fact, some corporations promote "computer training" to cure ADHD or to greatly help focus and attention. These companies charge up to $10,000 per year for "treatments" that aren't evidence-based.

If you find yourself worn out and giving up the fight, I understand. I get it. I have been there myself, and I've talked with countless parents walking down the same road. When parenting becomes challenging—or let's face it, unbearable—it's the most natural thing in the world to look for a way out, to avoid the issues, yell at your child, and search for an "easy" button. The "easy" button just doesn't exist.

> # THE PATH AHEAD IS NOT IN LOOKING FOR THE IMPOSSIBLE CURE BUT IN EMBRACING YOUR CHILD'S ADHD AND MAKING A PERSONAL INVESTMENT IN THEIR LIFE.

The path ahead is not spending money looking for the impossible cure but embracing your child's ADHD and making a personal investment in their life. Finding a way forward involves much more than a doctor, a teacher, or anything a computer program can offer—it involves you, the parent—you are the most critical factor in your child's success.

The importance of parental involvement in a child's life is a documented medical and scientific fact, and this is especially true for the ADHD individual. If you are not currently fighting for your child, it's time to get back in the fight. You are the one responsible for creating the emotional security and well-being of your child, instilling confidence, and unlocking their potential. You are the one responsible for implementing a strategy, tracking benchmarks, and seeing a plan through. No one knows your child like you do. You best understand them, what frustrates and inspires them, and how to effectively communicate with them. As your child grows and develops physically, mentally, and socially, no one has as much influence over them and their future as you do.

FastBraiin is not going to do the "work" for you, but our program is here to support you in the work—or the battle—and that's what it is, with wins and losses, with incredible sacrifice and incredible joys. It is a real battle to be fought, and it requires you—engaged and fighting with a full set of armor.

If that leaves you feeling overwhelmed, take a deep breath. We've seen too many success stories for you to count yourself out. Parents were created to make a difference in their children's lives. With a little direction, strategy, and perseverance, you can leverage your unique abilities and skills as a parent for the benefit of your child.

Our society sets the word "hero" aside for those who do random acts of bravery or for people who put themselves in harm's way to serve others. While we should honor those heroes, one of the most selfless and bravest acts a person can do today is to lead their family through life. The heroism is not in the one-time exertion of strength but in the consistent, often very ordinary acts of love and sacrifice that happen on a daily basis. It's not very flashy, and a newspaper may not cover your story, but to your child—and that's who this is really about—you mean the world!

Children do not have knowledge of ADHD, nor do they understand what issues may exist with their thinking and behavior. They require a leader, a teacher, a guide, and an encourager. Most of all, they need a hero. Who better to be their hero than you?

By transferring the burden of responsibility from outside the home to inside the home, not depending on the providers, educators, and programs, parents can take center stage. Only then can we lay a proper foundation and implement an effective strategy.

BECOMING A HERO FOR YOUR CHILD

Becoming a hero can seem like a lofty ideal that's hard to reach, not because we are unwilling but because we don't see how it connects with our day-to-day lives. In the rest of this chapter, we will discuss five primary ways you can become a hero for your child: believe in your child, lead by example, stay positive, learn from mistakes, and share the responsibility.

1. Believe in Your Child

At the beginning of the 2016 football season, almost everyone disregarded and discounted the Clemson Tigers. No one thought they would amount to much. Someone even made a YouTube video of all the TV commentators who didn't give the Tigers a chance. However, they went on to win the national championship. When reporters asked the head coach, Dabo Swinney, how they pulled it off, he remarked, "No one believed in these guys. But I did, and they believed in each other!"

The Clemson Tigers won because someone believed in them, inspired them to believe in themselves, gave them a strategy, and helped them carry out a plan of action.

Imagine the football squad if their coach didn't think they'd amount to much. Imagine if their coach decided to let them make their own schedule and run their own plays. It would be chaotic. But instead, their coach took charge—setting the tone for their attitudes, implementing a strategy, and inspiring them with hope for a national championship. For the players, it meant the journey of winning started the day after their last loss the previous year. It was a call to rise to the challenge, to make mistakes and correct them, and to do whatever it took to improve their performance. They accepted criticism while continuing to improve, supporting each other, and forcing themselves to give 100% to the big-picture goal. Ultimately, they forged themselves into a team that won the 2016 National Championship game by driving nearly 70 yards and making a pass with one second remaining to win. The team would have been a disaster had their previous mistakes defined them and if their coach had not believed in them. Instead, with a strong belief in what was possible, beginning with the coach, they accomplished more than anyone could have imagined. The Tigers would go on to win the national title again in 2019, solidifying their program and setting them up for years of success.

And that's what you are called to do. Your first step as a

parent is to believe in your child. That begins by making a shift in how you view your child—not seeing them as ADHD and going nowhere but instead as FastBraiin with a bright future. There is nothing more powerful than taking this initial step, leading the way by simply believing in your child. At first you may be thinking, "Of course I believe in my child!" But here's the deeper question: Does your child feel like you believe in them?

If you believe in your child with your head but functionally don't provide any evidence for this belief, then guess what? Your child does not know you believe in them. They can't read your mind; they can only read your actions. You might say you love and accept your child, but when the negative note comes home from the teacher, and you respond with anger and frustration, you communicate an entirely different message. Your child does not like upsetting you. They desire to please you, and the greater the love they have for you, the greater will be their pain and frustration when they disappoint you.[15]

The messages that our children hear come primarily through our emotions. Their emotional antennas are always raised, listening to not only what we say but how we say it. That's why we must be careful about our emotional responses to their actions. Our emotions speak louder than our words, and our children cultivate the same emotions we portray.

If we are always anxious about their school performance, they pick up on this and begin to feel anxious about it as well. If we are excited about learning, chances are they will get excited too. Growing and learning become opportunities for children to excel, not opportunities for them to grow anxious. Our emotions transfer into their emotions, and this means there is a tremendous amount of shaping we can do with our children simply by choosing to be positive and supportive.

THE DEEPER QUESTION IS: "DOES YOUR CHILD FEEL LIKE YOU BELIEVE IN THEM?"

This requires constant self-control and self-monitoring. Children are excellent at reading faces. We should keep the big picture in mind to temper our emotional responses. It's not worth it to emotionally lose it when your child gets a bad report card in the fourth grade. That causes your child to shut down. Instead, give your child a path forward. Focus on what they did well and how they can do better next time.

Responding positively also preserves and deepens the parent-child relationship, fostering an environment that is marked by safety. This opens the door for the child to be able to learn and grow without the fear of failure and to move forward with hope even when life is frustrating and challenging. Choosing to be positive does not change your child's FastBraiin—that's who they are—but shows them how to accept themselves, adapt to their environment, utilize their strengths, and develop a positive self-image.

I know this raises the bar for us as parents, but nobody ever said parenting was going to be easy, especially parents of Fast-Braiin kids! It's easy to place blame outside the home, pointing the finger at a doctor or a teacher; it's much harder to consider how we as parents might be part of the problem and what changes we might need to make. Success comes when we take this level of ownership.

Heroes in Action: Sean's Story
Sean and his mother came to see me in 2015. This 17-year-old loved football, and his six-foot-four, 240-pound frame fit him well

for the sport. Unfortunately, his grades weren't good enough to allow him to play. His parents were frustrated. Sean was frustrated. Life at home and school was tough. After listening to his personal story, it was evident Sean was feeling like a failure and feeling the disappointment of his parents.

When we discussed what he was most passionate about—cooking—he became excited. He wanted to be a chef, and he wanted to go to culinary school.

His mom, who was sitting with us in the appointment, quickly silenced that kind of "out of reach" talk by reminding him, "You aren't doing well in school. How do you expect to get into a culinary school? Let's be realistic about what you can do."

I then turned to Sean and said, "We will help you learn how to learn and focus so that you can improve your grades, go to college, and maybe even business school. You can be a chef and own the restaurant."

His eyes lit up. "You would help me do that?"

"Absolutely."

He then looked at his mom and said, "Please help me get the help I need from Dr. Jim so I can go to college."

Fast-forward a year later, when Sean and his mom came in for an office visit. There was quite a difference in our conversation. He had made the A/B honor roll, his football team had won the state title, and he had played so well that several colleges recruited him. "Thanks for all you have done for me, Dr. Jim," he said when he came in to tell me he was going to be playing college football. The exciting thing for me was to feel his emotion and to know that all I did was believe in him and show him a path forward.

The FastBraiin approach worked with Sean, mainly because his dad and mom became heroes in his life. They changed their home: they reinvented their household with changes in diet, sleep routine, screen time, and study skills. They began believing in and empowering Sean through their own emotions, words, and actions. In doing so, they also formed a positive emotional bridge between Sean and school via his long-term dreams of playing football and being a chef.

Sean's dad recently came to see me and thanked me for the restored relationship that he now has with his son. That conversation was music to my ears! I thanked him for believing in his son and helping him succeed. If Sean's parents had remained on the sidelines unable, unwilling, or just unsure about how to step in and get involved, Sean wouldn't have progressed. He needed their support, love, and accountability to begin moving in the right direction. And once they got locked in, Sean's confidence, direction, and hope for the future opened up to him.

> # SOME PARENTS HAVE TO FACE THE HARD REALIZATION THAT WHAT THEY ARE DOING IS WORKING AGAINST THEIR CHILD, NOT FOR THEIR CHILD.

We see this time and time again in our office. Many parents simply don't realize they aren't supporting and encouraging their child. Some have to face the hard realization that what they are doing is working against their child, not for their child. But once they come to grips with this reality, change is possible, and the exciting journey can begin.

A lot of times we as parents act negatively toward our children because we are anxious about their happiness and success. We've surveyed more than 1,000 parents at our bimonthly parent seminars over the last two years, and to our surprise, we have seen a consistent theme concerning parents' wishes for their kids. For moms, their number-one desire is they want their kids to be happy. For dads, their number-one desire is they want their kids to be successful.

There's nothing wrong with these desires, but the problem is in how parents go about trying to achieve them. We project our desires strongly on our children, overwhelming them and putting pressure on them that they can't handle. Kids just want to be kids, but the stresses and anxieties of their parents prevent them from exploring and learning in critical stages of development. And what does our level of anxiety and fear about our kids say about how much we believe in them? Barry Foote, former MLB star, comments on this reality: "Having played and coached at every level of baseball, from the juniors to the World Series, I understand that only a select few make it to the big leagues. What I have seen is that in nearly every case, those who make it are uniformly supported, not driven, by their parents."

Let's make sure that we truly believe in our kids, and then let's do everything we can to help them know and feel that belief in the ways we love, support, and cultivate *their* desires, not our own.

2. Lead by Example

Leading is hard, especially when you don't think you can lead or have become discouraged with the results. Leading is a full-time job. You never get a break from your children looking to you for direction. They don't just follow you on some days; they follow you every day. They are always watching your actions and reactions.

Kids learn how to act, how to show emotion, and what to do in their environment by following your example. If you aren't leading them, their behavior will reflect the culture around them. Unfortunately, our culture is not waiting to see what you will do—it's already fighting for your child's allegiance, and there is a lot in our culture that can be quite destructive. The influence that TV and peers have on your child is incredibly strong. Because our kids are naturally designed to follow, it's imperative that you as the parent present a positive, supportive example and strive to connect well with your child.

The good news is that kids are wired to look up to you. Every human instinctively looks first to their parents as their role model. Leading well does not mean being perfect. Leading well means being an example that your child can follow. They need to see you battle through life, work with limitations, adapt to your environment, apologize for wrongdoing, and bounce back from mistakes. There's no reason to hide these "less than perfect" moments from our children because these are teachable moments. When you apologize to your child for your emotions and mistakes, you model to them the act of apologizing and the need for taking responsibility, and you reinforce to your child that it's okay if they aren't perfect (because you aren't perfect). What matters is how we move forward.

Recognize that your kids listen to what you say and watch what you do. Words can tear down your kids or lift them up. As the parent, show your kids their value by how you talk to them, talk about them, and interact with them.

3. Stay Positive

When your child frustrates or disappoints you, try not to let those emotions be the first ones they see from you. Your emotions will become their emotions. Your kids will drive you crazy sometimes, but when you let emotions drive your response in those moments, you're not the hero they need you to be.

So how are you supposed to respond? Instead of instantly jumping on every mistake your child makes, remind them of the things they do right. You need to correct errors, but you don't need to dwell on their mistakes. If you do, your kids will begin to embody the negatives and see themselves in that negative shadow.

Acknowledge that we all have weaknesses and failures, and teach your child that it's a part of being human. Once you correct them about something they did or didn't do, there is no need to return to it time and time again. Let the lesson be learned, and don't hold it over their heads any longer. Stop telling them day in and day out what they can't do or what they should be doing. Instead, start praising the behaviors that you want to see developed. Point out the successes, no matter how small they seem. Encourage them in what they love to do.

In ADHD individuals, usually 80–90% of their self-talk is negative. That means as parents, we need to be much more positive than negative in what we say.

Their attention span is such that we have them tuned in to us for only 10–20 seconds. If we aren't boring or preachy, we may earn another 90 seconds. Keep your comments short, simple, and positive. Children need their home to be a refuge, not a war zone. A refuge is a place characterized by safety, support, and nourishment. A war zone is a place marked by threats, attacks, and pain. If your home is not a refuge, where else will your child go?

> # CHILDREN NEED THEIR HOME TO BE A REFUGE, NOT A WAR ZONE.

Do you spend more time focusing on the negatives or the positives of your child's behavior? Imagine a big whiteboard that keeps a tally of all the positive and all the negative comments you make to your child. How often does your child hear, "I love you,"

"That was a super play you made in the game," "I'm proud of you," "You are such a hard worker," or "I enjoy spending time with you"? If you are like most parents, our negatives significantly outweigh the positives, which serve to reinforce and cultivate our child's negative internal dialogue.

Unfortunately, it takes many more positive affirmations to undo the negatives. For this reason, it is vitally important that parents monitor their speech. Words can hurt deeply. If you think you're using more negative words, being honest with yourself is the best place to start. Only when we face the reality of our negative tendencies can we begin adjusting toward a more positive approach. Getting and staying positive—loving and accepting your child—may be the most significant factor in your child's success. When you are being positive, point out the specific action. Instead of saying, "You played a great game," tell them, "The kick you made in the third quarter was awesome!"

Dr. Hallowell believes: "It is love, wise love, smart love, persistent and unremitting love that they need, first and foremost."

Fig. 3.0

I particularly like how he goes on to say:

> *For love to do its transformative work . . . it must not be blind. It must see clearly and be brave . . . [you must see] without illusion the child who stands before you, the child you actually have, as opposed to the child you always wanted or wished you had, and you love that child, the messy child, the child who doesn't win the prizes or get the lead role, the child who doesn't get top grades and who isn't necessarily headed for an Ivy League school, the child who can't play the instrument you wanted her to play, who can't throw the fastball you wanted him to throw, nor was ever meant to. . . . More than anything else, it is love that separates those who thrive in life from those who do not.*"[16]

Showing this type of unconditional, unrelenting love to your child is the stuff of heroes.

Researchers conducted one study on a group of students, examining the correlation between their grades and how parents addressed them, either positively or negatively. The study showed that when parents spoke to their children in a positive manner at least 50% of the time, they did significantly better socially and in school than in cases where children heard more than 50% negative talk. Listen to how you talk to your child. Try listing your positive and negative statements throughout the day. You may be surprised at what you find.

Choosing not to dwell on negativity is one of the sacrifices that a hero and a leader must make, and that can be difficult, especially when you don't feel positive yourself. Work on keeping the big picture in mind. If you need to vent, vent with your spouse or with a trusted friend, but keep it away from your child. You need to set the tone and be the hero. But being positive does not mean turning a blind eye to problematic behavior and sweeping it under the rug. You need to confront your child. They need to know they have stepped across the line. It's a disservice to your child if you set boundaries and allow them to cross over them without consequences. It's even more of a disservice if you don't set any boundaries at all. An F is not really an A, and pretending everything is okay confuses your child and prevents them from maturing. ADHD kids not only need boundaries, they thrive with them.

> # ADHD KIDS NOT ONLY NEED BOUNDARIES, THEY THRIVE WITH THEM.

Your child is a stallion—a racehorse, not a plow horse. They need boundaries, they need a fence, but then they need to run, so let them go. We just need to help them focus and give them some boundaries. And then we sit back and watch them run! We don't need to try to turn them into plow horses—that minimizes each horse's unique strengths.

So set firm boundaries, and address them when your child breaks them. The positive or negative aspect occurs in how you confront them. You can choose to criticize and tear down, or you can be constructive and build up. Be honest about their behavior and the consequences, but frame it in terms of why that particular behavior is harmful, why you asked them to behave differently, what they can learn from it, and how they can do better next time.

Consider it your challenge to find something good in every situation. Even if your child makes an F on a test, your job is still to see the A within them. Was there a section they did well on?

Did they learn something interesting? How can the study method be tweaked to do better next time? Your job is to dig for and focus on the positives. If they made a bad grade, let's learn from it and figure out how to improve!

Just like you know the importance of timing in having a serious conversation with your spouse or boss, make sure that you are choosing the best time and place to speak to your child. If you think you are about to "lose it" emotionally, excuse yourself from the room and take a few deep breaths. You can always return to the subject at another time. Work through your emotions on your own before you work through them with your child. Remember, your responses will help shape who they become. It's always better to have constructive talks in private, without the fear of public embarrassment or shame. If it's a positive conversation, public affirmation is great and will go a long way to encourage your child.

4. Learn from Mistakes

A quarterback will throw an interception, a batter will get out more than he'll get on base, and a tennis player in the finals of the US Open will lose over 40% of the points. Michael Jordan only made 44% of the shots he ever took, but he's remembered as one of the greatest basketball players of all time. But we don't harp on these momentary failures. No, we wait to see if the athlete will pull through in the overall performance. Why don't we view our children this way?

The father of a 10-year-old patient was recently in the office, and we were discussing his son's basketball ability. This dad played college basketball, and in his mind, his son was making mistakes that were unacceptable. I asked the dad about his own story, and as he shared about his basketball journey, I asked him if he ever made mistakes. Naturally, his answer was yes. Next, I asked him which he learned more from, his successes or his mistakes.

He had an "aha" moment, realizing what he was doing with his child when he called out "the mistakes." Mistakes can be our best teachers, but only if we are allowed to make them and we are open to learning from them. Our education system does not think in these terms, and we as parents don't do much better. We tend to view our children's learning as static, with a fixed level of smartness or dumbness. We let grades and IQ tests label our kids for life.

Robert Sternberg, former President and Professor of Psychology and Education at the University of Wyoming, boldly proposes a new horizon: choosing to consider learning and intelligence on a continuum, which he calls dynamic learning. The reason is simple. Static learning, characterized by standardized tests, "is limited to a static report of where we are on the learning continuum at the time the test is given. . . . [They tell us] only what we know at any given moment . . . and nothing about our potential."[17]

Peter Brown and others add that in dynamic learning, "a test may assess a weakness, but rather than assuming that the weakness indicates a fixed inability, you interpret it as a lack of skill or knowledge that can be remedied."[18] In this type of learning, mistakes are the gateway to deep learning and to reaching one's potential. This view intentionally chooses not to label kids but to see them on a continuum and always developing. Dynamic learning "holds that with continued experience in a field we are always moving from a lower state of competence to a higher one."[19]

When children no longer fear mistakes as judges, but embrace them as teachers, the learning process opens up to them. Parents need to, therefore, help their children properly view and learn from their mistakes. Mistakes are teachers, not judges. When we answer incorrectly in class and are corrected, it is amazing how that learning experience tends to stick.

Why Failing Matters: Earl's Story

Earl was in the eleventh grade and a super kid, but he had little self-esteem, even though he was a football star at the local high school. It seems most boys have their true self-esteem developed not through sports but through academic performance. Earl was a D/F student in the eighth, ninth, and tenth grades, and this put his eligibility in question for his senior year.

We had a great first meeting at our FastBraiin clinic. Earl also saw our educational specialist and psychologist, and we established a game plan. His parents took on the challenge of implementing significant changes at home and school, as did Earl. He returned several months later with a big smile, with all A's and B's on his report card. I stood up, stepped toward this fantastic young man, but before I could hug him, tears were already coming down his face. Then the words came out that caused me to also become emotional, "Dr. Jim, I'm okay!"

The bottom line for why we must not respond negatively to our children when they make mistakes is that children internalize our responses and begin believing they aren't okay. This belief drives down their self-esteem and motivation, which leads to more errors, reinforcing their negative belief patterns. When we allow children to make mistakes and positively correct them, we stop the negative cycle and help them move forward.

5. Share the Responsibility

Finally, to walk as a hero, you need to realize that real heroes don't go it alone. Solo missions rarely succeed, and this is especially true in parenting. Parenting is hard, and we often get discouraged and beaten down by everyday life. To keep your energy and strength up, and to continue being the hero for your kids, make sure you have a support group around you. Your support network can include your spouse, friends, neighbors, relatives, teachers, counselors, doctors, and coaches. Lean on them. Don't be afraid to ask for help.

And don't bottle up your emotions and discouragement. As a leader, you cannot put your adverse reactions on display for your kids, but neither can you ignore them or wish them away. Take your struggles and discouragement to your support network, not your kids. Lean on other adults in your life who can help share the burden of your struggles. If your support network is unable to help you manage your negative emotions, it may be necessary to seek professional counseling.

SUMMARY

- Every FastBraiin child needs a hero.
- Parents are best suited and most needed to be their child's hero.
- Parents become heroes by believing in their child, leading by example, relating positively to their child's ADHD, and seeing mistakes as learning opportunities.
- Mistakes help us learn and grow. Mistakes are teachers, not judges.
- Being a hero does not mean going it alone. Parents are encouraged to share the joy and the responsibility of parenting with others, as well as finding or developing a support network.

CHAPTER 4

FLIPPING EDUCATION, PART I

How to Increase
Learning at Home

*"Study habits at home are the differentiator
between students who succeed and those
who struggle."*

We started this book asking you to flip your thinking about ADHD, which is the essential first step toward developing an adequate approach. Now it's time to get started on one of the leading issues of ADHD—education. The majority of children and parents who come to our FastBraiin clinics come because of learning issues. Though behavior problems may exist in the home, rarely does someone seek out ADHD help until problems surface in the classroom, with most concerns focusing on grades.

The reason for low grades is that within the current medical and education systems, there is a discrepancy between how we currently understand the ADHD brain and how we teach students. In the typical medical journey, the health provider gives the patient a survey and sends them to an expensive psychologist for ADHD testing. The report then comes back to the provider with the diagnosis, and the patient is put on medication—all without providing a single learning strategy or tracking an individual's outcomes.

A similar process plagues our education system. Many educators, in their efforts to "fix" ADHD children, often unknowingly damage their self-esteem, thereby disrupting their learning process and alienating them from their peers. Teachers put their names on the board, keep them in from recess, send them to the principal's office, and even suspend them from school. How do you think this makes them feel? Not very good, right? And imagine what this does to the child's internal learning environment. Ironically, teachers create chaos rather than cultivate the child's internal learning environment.

Things are no better when suspended students return to school. Teachers and health care providers haven't been taught how to help individuals who have issues with attention, focus, and behavior. Their attempts to correct behavior make ADHD symptoms worse, not better. They don't understand that singling out an ADHD child, or keeping them from recess, shuts down their ability to learn and focus. These negative forces compound the negativity that the child already experiences.

THERE IS A DISCREPANCY BETWEEN HOW WE CURRENTLY UNDERSTAND THE ADHD BRAIN AND HOW WE TEACH STUDENTS.

As parents, we aren't much better. We send them to their room to do homework but don't periodically check in. We mostly remain absent from their educational journey. Home life is disorganized and stressful. The average home has several TVs or screens on at any given time. And we as parents are constantly checking our phones, texting, or browsing the web, which creates an environment that works against our child's ability to focus and learn. If parents are fortunate enough to know some useful study skills, they often don't take the time and energy to implement them.

The good news is that with a few simple techniques and adjustments, your child can experience significant learning gains at home and in school. Each setting has its unique environment, set of challenges, and protocol for success. Some students work well at school and do poorly at home, and vice versa. The breakdown, however, is usually at home. The study habits at home are the differentiator between students who succeed and those who struggle. We parents have a degree of control over what happens at home, whereas we can't control what goes on at school.

With this in mind, we will start with how to improve learning at home, and then in chapter 5 we will consider how to improve learning in the classroom.

Strategies for Learning at Home

The six most effective strategies we recommend at FastBraiin for increased learning at home are:

1. Establish an Emotionally Encouraging Learning Environment

We share this technique first because it is of paramount importance. Nothing is as critical to your child's learning as creating an environment that is emotionally encouraging.

The brain is incredibly complex; the more we learn about the brain, the more we realize how much we don't know. Medical books and websites are regularly updated with thousands of pages of new information. For instance, Mark Bear has recently published *Neuroscience: Exploring the Brain* (1,008 pages), and Russell Barkley, MD, has edited *Assessment of Mental Disorders* (877 pages). We are in the midst of a massive explosion of new information about the brain.

Given this complexity, it's surprising that certain groups and programs promise quick fixes for ADHD—at the cost of $10,000 in some cases—claiming to change brain chemistry, improve IQ, and turn ADHD children into successful individuals. At this point, there have been no medical studies or FDA approval backing any such claims.

We all want a quick fix. It's part of human nature. But to best help ourselves and our kids, especially when it comes to education, we should keep this in mind: there is no test for ADHD, there is no quick fix for ADHD, and there is no cure for ADHD. But the complexity and difficulty of ADHD doesn't mean that we are powerless; it implies that change takes time, effort, and understanding.

I was in Washington, DC, a few years ago at a CHADD conference (Children and Adults with ADD) and decided to go to a breakout session on brain mapping and brain disorders. A neuroscientist and psychiatrist at the University of Chicago was speaking. Knowing it was going to be boring, my FastBraiin brain told me to sit in the back for 30 minutes and then leave.

Though she was an unquestionable academic, she was

fascinating! Amazingly, I stayed for three hours, listening to her share that she had mapped out more than 1,000 emotional pathways in the brain. These emotional channels connect to our prefrontal cortex, our learning center, and areas associated with our senses. The neuroscientist's talk about learning issues did not include anything about being out of balance between left and right brain hemispheres but instead focused on the need to cultivate emotional pathways, and that such pathways develop differently within each brain. Her conclusion was that all parts of the brain are interwoven and interconnected to emotion—which is central to learning.

Consider the "fight-or-flight" response in the body that takes place when there is a perceived threat.

What is happening in the brain? Our prefrontal cortex (thinking area) produces a thought and sends a signal to our amygdala (emotional center), which then sends a signal to our limbic system. The limbic system then sends a signal to our adrenal glands, which increases our cortisol and, in turn, increases our heart rate and blood pressure. All of this happens instantly so we can fight the enemy at hand or run away. When our brain undergoes this process, it is working well, and we are thankful for it when we need it. When running from a tiger, who couldn't use a little bit more adrenaline? But when trying to learn, stress hormones make things worse.

Any perceived threat will cause stress levels to rise, whether it's a tiger, teacher, or an upset parent. Threats, pressures, and stresses undo positive emotion for children and can come in any form. It could happen when they are scolded for not cleaning their room, when a note from the teacher comes home, when they make a bad grade, when faced with social pressures, or when there is parental conflict in the home. Ever wonder why your child argues with you or runs away from you? Their fight-or-flight system is in high gear.

Note also that there is not a "Thanks, Mom, for pointing that out—can we sit quietly and discuss the issue?" center in our brain!

When our child's emotional system is on high alert, what are the chances that they want to sit down and do their homework or have a nice family dinner? And what are the chances of you, the parent, going to bed happy?

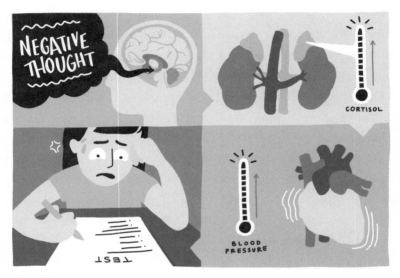

Fig. 4.0

The rise of negative emotions helps explain why your child does not want to go to school the next day. School is a threat because it causes stress. It takes serious guts for a child with ADHD, who has been scolded by their teacher and parents, to get up, get dressed, and head back to school. And the cycle goes on and on. Not fun.

Therefore, we should strive to create an environment that cultivates positive emotions in you and in your child. You will need to focus on your relationship with your child. What is the emotional environment of your relationship? Pursue your child. Get to know your child. Do they feel accepted by you? Are they able to talk to you about their problems? Or are they afraid of what you might say and do?

Consider other variables in the home that disrupt positive emotion. What is the parent-to-parent interaction like? How does your child interact with siblings? Is your schedule chaotic? Do you eat breakfast and dinner together, and if you do, is it in front of the TV where there is little to no communication? Is your home disorganized and cluttered? Each of these variables, when considered on its own, may not amount to much, but the cumulative effect can significantly alter your child's ability to learn.

Clutter in our surroundings has the effect of cluttering our mind. We go to a Parade of Homes tour and exclaim how each room is beautiful and the homes feel so peaceful. What we don't see is clutter! Hundreds of articles are written by organization gurus touting the calming effect of a clean desk in the morning when you start work. This means you need to clean the desk prior to leaving the night before. In my office, I have big windows that look out onto a busy parking lot. I have my desk facing a wall with one picture of a calm scene and an adjacent wall with three pictures of personal importance. All are calming and relaxing and help me with my focus and attention on the task at hand. Make an effort to have your child's workspace free from clutter.

Being positive is not just about removing stress and negativity; it's about actually being positive. Your language and behavior must encourage and build your child's confidence. Developing their confidence in their ability to succeed—whether in giving a speech, taking a test, writing an essay, or playing a sport—allows them the freedom to make mistakes and continue learning.

Some neuroscientists argue that the single most critical factor in one's ability to learn is the belief that they *can* learn. Researchers performed a study in which they taught one group of children that the brain was fixed, and they taught another group of children that the brain had an ability to adapt and learn. Then they gave both groups a set of problems to solve. The group that believed they could learn and improve significantly outperformed the group that thought their intelligence was fixed.[20]

CONFIDENCE CAN'T BE GIVEN; IT'S SOMETHING THAT MUST BE EARNED.

Confidence can't be given; it's something that must be earned. You can help develop it, but you can't force it. A baseball player must hit the ball to believe they can hit. So, if you want them to learn how to hit the ball, what do you do? You start with placing the ball on a tee, then you move up to slow pitch, and so on. Even if they end up hitting a 95-mph fastball in college, they still needed to start with hitting on the tee to develop their confidence and ability.

And the same process has to happen with education! We can tell kids they are FastBraiin, that they are gifted and intelligent, which will get them moving down the positive pathway. But it's quite another thing when a FastBraiin child comes home with their first A on a report card. At that point, confidence skyrockets. If you can instill in your children confidence in who they are and confidence that they can learn, then you have done a wonderful job!

2. Create a Homework Routine

Homework is usually an extremely stressful time for the entire family. To change your child's learning environment at home, you must establish a productive routine. Scattered schedules make scattered brains. "While we all need external structure in our lives—some degree of predictability, routine, organization," says Dr. Hallowell, "those with ADD need it much more than most people. They need external structure so much because they so lack internal structure."[21]

Setting routines is about setting the external structure and, therefore, the internal structure for your child. Routines that your child learns to expect and embrace will have a direct influence on their focus, mood, decision-making, and overall productivity.

As you consider what routine works best for your ADHD child, make sure you think about it with the rest of the family in mind. The only way to move forward and sustain your child's rhythms over the long term is to integrate the plan well within the family. Chart out the weekly schedule for each person. Set specific study times that are free from distractions (like having the TV on). If you must watch TV, use earphones, but remember that leading by example takes priority.

> ## SCATTERED SCHEDULES MAKE SCATTERED BRAINS.

The weekly schedule also includes having a set time to do homework or review work each night. There's no such thing as "no homework." That only means no new work was assigned. Every night there is homework because every night is review night.

Setting expectations ahead of time and developing a plan reduces the possibility of stressors that create strife when trying to settle down and study at home.

Part of the after-school routine should allow time and space for decompression as well. Before starting on homework after school, let your child expend some energy. Keep in mind that when your child comes home from school, they have been sitting and focusing for hours. They deserve and need a little time to decompress, just like you do when you get home from work. I recommend at least 30 minutes to an hour of decompression time before starting again on mentally demanding tasks.

Any movement will suffice for expending energy—from running a few laps around the house, jumping rope, swinging, or playing with a friend to participating in an after-school sport or favorite activity. Finally, as a transition period, give your child a healthy snack and a glass of water before they return to learning mode. Stay away from sugary fruit drinks and sodas.

Once your child is refreshed, encourage them to start homework with their most difficult subject first. Make sure you build breaks into their homework routine. Your child can't work like a machine, and their mind and emotions need short breaks to refuel. Your child should take a break from studying every 20–25 minutes. This break can be a quick 50 jumping jacks, running in place, or push-ups, followed by a glass of water (see chapter 8). You will have to tailor this break time to your child's attention cycle.

THE AFTER-SCHOOL ROUTINE SHOULD ALLOW TIME AND SPACE FOR DECOMPRESSION.

Having a homework routine is nice, but what happens when your child does everything *but* their homework? Procrastination is a common enemy that plagues all of us. Our next strategy shows how you can turn your procrastinating kids into productivity all-stars.

3. Turn Procrastination into Productivity

One of the most significant obstacles to learning is procrastination. We put off doing schoolwork, delay studying, and then cram our brains for the test, only to forget everything as we walk out the door. Procrastination is an enemy of effective learning, productivity, and reaching one's potential.

Have you ever walked into your child's room and wondered why they were playing video games or drawing and not doing their homework? And then you find out that the test is tomorrow, or that the project is due in two days, and you realize there is no way your child is going to be ready for the test or can finish the project. The reason is simple—video games and drawing are more fun than doing homework.

Before we get too upset with our kids, we need to realize that we have these same behavioral patterns. We constantly put off what we need to do, don't we? We do "other" stuff that might be important but is not a priority, ignoring the one thing that needs to get done. It's just more fun to clean out our desk or check our email than to get back to the task at hand.

OUR BRAIN'S PAIN CENTER

To fight procrastination, we need to understand a little about how the brain works. We have an area of our brain that scientists refer to as the pain center. As you might have guessed by the name, this is the area of our brain that feels pain. Within the last two years, neuroscientists have discovered that we also have a procrastination center. At a recent APSARD (The American Professional Society of ADHD and Related Disorders) meeting, a neuroscientist from Stanford showed us where the pain and procrastination areas exist in the brain. To everyone's surprise, the procrastination center and the pain center overlap, which means they are in the same place. So it makes sense why we feel pain when we're procrastinating—it's painful! And it's also why your child wants to play video games instead of doing their homework. Reward center or pain center—which would you choose?

When we procrastinate, we are avoiding pain. When I sit down to do patient medical charting (which I hate doing), I usually procrastinate. I go in circles trying to avoid doing them: I might get water, check emails, make a phone call, get up and walk around, check more emails, and clean my desk. The circle of frustration goes on and on.

Think about how you feel when you start something you don't want to do. You first must fight through the pain of getting started. But after a few minutes of working and doing the "chore," the pain subsides, and you might even begin enjoying the activity. It's like when you pinch yourself on the arm, you will notice that after about 15–30 seconds you will no longer focus on the pain. Your brain has shifted its focus. When I finally sit down and begin going through my charts, I realize it's not so bad. And before long, I'm getting them done.

Your child doesn't want to do homework because they don't want to feel pain. It's a battle between their reward center and their pain center. They see threat and difficulty in the task they should be doing (homework), and they perceive ease and pleasure in the things they shouldn't be doing (video games, Instagram).

Fig. 4.1

It may be helpful to consider what types of pain or threat they experience when procrastinating. If we can isolate why they are avoiding their work, we might be able to lessen the threat and increase the likelihood that they study. Although there are countless reasons for procrastination and pain, a few we regularly see in the office include—

1. **I do not know the material well enough.**
    (pain/threat of feeling inadequate or stupid)

2. **It is going to be hard to do.**
    (pain/threat of being frustrated)

3. **I would rather do something else.**
    (pain/threat of missing out on pleasure)

4. **It is not going to work.**
    (pain/threat of wasting time)

5. I don't think I can do it.
(pain/threat of being a failure)

In light of these painful, threatening situations, our children naturally choose other, more promising paths to pleasure with less pain or threat involved. Procrastination is an attempt to find pleasure without the risk. This can feed the ADHD mind, which already tends toward obsessive compulsivity. They search for reward and pleasure by putting off what they should be doing.

Just like an addiction, they escape into video games, social media, or anything else that brings immediate pleasure. If only they could realize that the joy and pleasure they really want is not achieved through avoidance but by facing and overcoming their pain head-on.

The good news is that with the right strategies and techniques, helping your child overcome procrastination is not nearly as hard as one might think. In general, the best strategies are to "trick" the brain into not perceiving pain while also increasing the perception of pleasure—which is what ultimately stands between your child and their studying.

1. Utilize the Pomodoro Technique

Francesco Cirillo developed this classic technique in the 1980s. The word *"pomodoro"* comes from a tomato-shaped kitchen timer that he used (*pomodoro* is Italian for tomato). In this technique, you intentionally shorten the scope and intensity of the work to be done. For example, writing an essay may be a daunting task when you consider how much mental energy and time it will take to complete it. The "bigness" of the task tends to overwhelm and paralyze you so that you never start. The Pomodoro technique breaks down the time and energy into bite-size, manageable chunks.

Set a timer for 20–25 minutes (some ADHD kids need even less, maybe 10 or 15 minutes). Decide on exactly what your child needs to accomplish in that chunk of time. Maybe the first step in writing an essay is for your child to write an outline. Start the timer and have your child commit to working on the outline for 20 minutes.

When the timer goes off, no matter where your child is on the assignment, make them get up and take a three-minute break (get a glass of water, shoot basketball outside, or do some jumping jacks). After the break, your child needs to come back and do another Pomodoro session with a new goal in mind.

The brain has a way of looking at a 20-minute block of time with the task of writing an outline as doable. It's certainly less painful and threatening than writing an entire essay. The Pomodoro technique is extremely effective at minimizing pain and busting through procrastination cycles.

2. Play Music

You may already use music to beat procrastination without even knowing it. It's quite natural to turn on the tunes when needing a little motivation for any activity. I personally use music when I have to log my charts, exercise, or work in the yard. It's amazing how fast the time can fly with music playing. Music stimulates the brain and fires up the pleasure center, increasing our motivation and distracting us from our experience of pain. In the same way, music helps your child fight through their pain when studying or doing homework.

In 2010, I took a group of 25 kids, 10–15 years old, put them in a room, and presented them with a timed math test. We started with a 10-minute test, done in silence (or as quietly as possible!). I then played an upbeat song, "Boogie Wonderland," from the movie *Happy Feet*, and asked them to do the 10-minute test again. The purpose was to measure how many problems they could answer correctly, with and without the added music.

As the kids were dancing and singing to the music during the test, I remember thinking that I might need to apologize to the parents who gave up their Saturday morning for this study. But before I got the chance, my nurse called me over to look at the scores. All the kids improved their score when the music was playing. One child did 34 problems and only got four correct without music, but when music was played, he did 44 problems and got all 44 correct! The pharmaceutical companies look for a 28% improvement in scores on medication as their success rate. Our scores went up an average of 38%! Playing music for ADHD children while they do their homework or take a test may improve their scores as much as or more than medication.

When it's time for your child to study, try playing music. Find out what genre works best for them as well as at what volume. Experiment. Develop a playlist that your child enjoys and finds helpful. Having a set playlist will cue your child's brain and reinforce to them that it's time to study. Any genre of music is fair game if it works, but we recommend staying away from hip-hop because of the verbal load on the brain.

Playing music while they are studying gives them a positive feeling, and it tricks the brain into thinking that they are doing something they enjoy!

3. Think Reward

As mentioned, the procrastination cycle is a battle of pain versus pleasure. The work we should be doing is painful, while the activities we find ourselves doing when procrastinating are pleasurable. The goal is not to minimize pain but to see pain as a stepping-stone to more pleasure.

The brain's focus is on the actual work involved in writing an essay, which can be overwhelming and produce a threat of pain. Instead of focusing on the workload, your child needs to fix their attention on some other aspect that they find pleasurable. Maybe it's the satisfaction of getting a good grade, or the goal of becoming a better writer, or of learning something new. It's the same concept that an athlete uses when going to the gym. An athlete who only focuses on lifting weights will soon get burned out, but an athlete who dreams of winning a championship will have an endless amount of motivation for extra sets and harder workouts.

> # THE GOAL IS NOT TO MINIMIZE PAIN BUT TO SEE PAIN AS A STEPPING-STONE TO MORE PLEASURE.

To build pleasure into the activity, look for ways of utilizing educational material that is relevant to the child. This will naturally engage their brain. If they need to learn to count and are into race cars, let them count race cars. If they need to write an essay and they love to dance, let them write about a type of dance. This will help them stay engaged and find value in what they're doing. Unless you are in a flexible environment, choosing the subject matter may not be possible. However, you can help teach and encourage through the use of analogy with their favorite subjects.

4. Exercise

People rarely turn to exercise to beat procrastination, but it's one of the most powerful tools in our toolbox. It works because exercise fires up the brain and gets the "feel good" neurotransmitters flowing. The pleasure your child experiences after exercising can translate into confidently tackling work that previously appeared unapproachable. Exercise increases blood flow, cognitive ability, confidence, and mood, all which translates into an ability to fight through procrastination. When you catch your child procrastinating, rebelling against doing work, or simply in a cognitive slump, have them run around outside for a bit, do some jumping jacks, or engage in some other heartbeat increasing activity. Then watch them break through procrastination and tackle their tasks. There are many more benefits to exercise than just beating procrastination. We will take a deeper look at its relationship to overall learning and health in chapter 6.

4. Use the FastBraiin Study Method: Engage, Retrieve, Repeat (ERR)

After finishing my pediatric residency in El Paso in 1979, the US Army deployed me to Germany, where I became chief of pediatrics. The Army took me as a young, insecure, uneducated physician with ADHD and, in three short years of residency, transformed me into a self-sufficient, headstrong doctor unafraid to try new things. How did they do that?

At each morning report, I had to turn in a written four-page summary and two articles relevant to each patient that I admitted to the hospital the day or night before. It was then that the fun began. I had 90 seconds—and only 90 seconds—to present a summary in front of 15 pediatric house staff (other MDs in training) and 15 staff physicians. Then they would fire questions at me for 10 minutes straight—some likened this to dart throwing—asking anything about the patient or the disease process, even asking questions from the articles that were attached, and I was expected to be able to discuss it all.

If I had been on call that night, I would have spent most of the evening caring for patients, and the rest of the time I spent preparing for those 90 seconds of fear and challenge. For three years this process continued, and by the end of it, everyone was confident in their knowledge and understanding.

During my third year of training, I was sent to do an externship at Duke University. While there, the fellow in Infectious Disease became sick, and the department head, Dr. Katz, allowed me to take his place. I had no idea how I would stand up educationally in this environment. However, to everyone's surprise—except for my Army staff physicians—I was on par with the Duke staff. My performance was not due to my innate ability to learn but because of the way I had been taught to learn by Colonel Fearnow.

Colonel Fearnow was the Chief of Pediatrics at William Beaumont Army Medical Center, and everyone who trained under him owes him a huge debt of gratitude. His way of educating and working us through three years of training resulted in every one of us passing our national boards and becoming successful pediatricians.

This study method took me from an inexperienced student to a knowledgeable physician in a short amount of time. I was not at the top in my medical school class, but learning this technique made all the difference in how I learn, even to this day, and has given me confidence and knowledge to maximize my passion and work as a FastBraiin pediatrician. My experience in the Army, combined with knowledge gained from recent neuroscience about the brain, has led to the development of the FastBraiin learning method.

The FastBraiin learning method involves three steps: engage, retrieve, and repeat. Each step is critical to the method's success.

Fig. 4.2

ENGAGE

The first step in your child's learning is for them to engage with their subject. If they are not going to class or not studying at home, they won't know the material at test time. The more actively engaged your child is with their study material, the greater impression that information will make in their brain, and the more likely they will understand and remember what's being taught. It's one thing to listen to a teacher lecture. It's quite another thing to take notes, share what you are learning with classmates, and apply the information to new contexts. The more deeply involved your child is with the material, the better. Incorporate different ways of learning: write it, say it, read it, discuss it, and even act it out, if possible.

ADHD brains are fast, very fast. It's this fast speed that allows us to process information and adapt to changing environments. It is also what often gets us into trouble because we quickly switch gears and become distracted with the next glittering object. Attention deficit disorder is not so much a lack of attention as it is attention described differently. The brain is so fast that it gets bored easily and looks for more engaging stimuli. Parents can use this to their advantage when it comes to maximizing engagement for their children.

> ## ATTENTION DEFICIT DISORDER IS NOT SO MUCH A LACK OF ATTENTION AS IT IS ATTENTION DESCRIBED DIFFERENTLY.

Try letting your child bounce from subject to subject: 15 minutes on math, for example, and then 15 minutes on English. Keeping the content fresh is a wonderful way to encourage attention and engagement, and this method actually makes learning occur at a deeper level. We recommend interval training for the brain, using small chunks of study time for optimal engagement. Have your child study for 15 or 20 minutes, and then have them take a break. If you see their focus wandering, as mentioned, have them do some jumping jacks or run in place, and then have them return to study.

Another way to increase engagement is to tap into your child's passions. What is relevant and meaningful to your child? Is it a sport, hobby, reading, or some other special interest? Use this information to help your child connect with subjects they find boring—be creative! The Olympic swimmer Michael Phelps had trouble focusing on math until his mom related his math problems to the swimming pool. He found the abstractness of mathematics boring, but when he had to solve problems about speed in water over distance, he became engaged. As the authors of *Fast Minds* write, "What someone pays attention to comes down to

interesting the options are, or the ability to get
rested in them."[22] Varying material, using interval
adjusting content for relevancy work together to
prolong attention by keeping interest up.

RETRIEVE

After your child has engaged with the subject and stored information in their brain, it's time to retrieve that information. If
there is one technique that will give your child the biggest bang
for their study time, it's this—to spend time retrieving information, testing themselves to see if they know it, and correcting
mistakes as they go.[23] This is the opposite of mindlessly reviewing, which many times makes us think we know something when
we really don't. Research has found that testing yourself out-
performs every other study technique because it reinforces the
development of myelin—meet your child's new best friend and
favorite study partner. Myelin is a fatty substance in the brain
that protects and establishes neural connections, which make
up our memories. The more myelin that surrounds a particular neuron and connection of neurons, the more solidified that
memory will be in the brain, and the faster that knowledge can
be retrieved. What's fascinating is that every time you recall or
review something, you deposit myelin in the brain and the connection strengthens. Merely reviewing material feels productive, but studies show that this feeling is an illusion. It is only
after testing yourself that you realize how much you really don't
know. With this type of practice, when it becomes test-taking
time, your child will be more than ready.

One of the best and easiest ways to utilize the technique of
retrieval is to make flashcards. There's a reason flashcards have
endured the test of time. Have your child review them from front
to back and back to front, if applicable. Online platforms like

Quizlet allow you to make virtual flashcard decks, along with several added features.

A study session that incorporates interval training, retrieval practices, and exercise might look like Fig. 4.3.

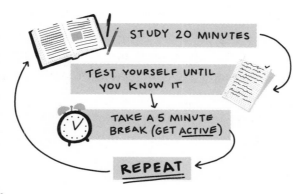

Fig. 4.3

REPEAT

We've engaged, we've retrieved, and now it's time to repeat the process. Repetition is absolutely critical to the formation of memory. The focus is still on forming strong neural pathways through the formation of myelin. With every repetition, myelin is applied and reinforced. It must be stressed again, however, that it is the repetition of a memory through recall (not mindlessly reviewing) that most efficiently builds myelin and solidifies a memory in the brain.

Musicians instinctively know the power of forming neural connections. They know that if they practice mistakes, they will soon make those errors in their performance. That's why the best training involves correcting errors as they happen and only going over a few notes at a time until they can perform them correctly. Practice does not make perfect—perfect practice makes perfect.

The same mechanism for memory formation is at work whether it's for a piano recital, developing muscle memory for dance, or memorizing a periodic table. The memory gets locked in place by myelin through repetition. Or think of it this way—every time you repeat something, it's like traveling a path through the jungle. At first, the path is hard to discern (and the memory is fuzzy), but after you travel the path a few times, the path becomes clearer. Repetition is like laying down gravel and then eventually paving a highway. Soon the path is super clear, and the memory solidifies.

I have a little trick that I do with my patients to teach them about myelin. I ask them, "What do I drive?"

They reply, "I don't know."

To this I say, "A red truck."

Then I ask them again, "What do I drive?"

"A red truck" comes back as the obvious answer.

And then I ask it again. And again. And again. (Six times)

The fun part is that after that, they never forget what color truck I drive, and the point is driven home to them (no pun intended). It's not that ADHD kids are stupid; it's that information is unfamiliar, and no one has taught them how to study. Repetition is critical to building myelin and strengthening connections. You want your child to have multiple exposures to whatever it is they are trying to learn.

Consider using repetition in a single study session. When it comes to reading, I suggest having your child skim a passage three times. It probably will take them the same amount of time it would usually take them to read it once. For instance, on the first read, have them go over all the headings and subheadings. On the second read, have them read the first and the last sentences of each paragraph. And on the third read, have them skim the entire material (Fig. 4.4). Try this technique yourself on a newspaper or magazine article. It's remarkable how much you can know about an article just by reading the headings, captions, and the first and last sentences. Your brain gathers all this information so that when you skim the entire article, you put your memory bank to work without conscious effort.

Fig. 4.4

You must also use repetition in multiple study sessions. Reviewing is the one thing we all know we should do, but don't do. It's hard (remember the pain center!). We trick ourselves into thinking we know the material, even though that assumption is false. The question is not if you know the information right now but if you will know it at test time. Reviewing takes extra work up front—but in the long run, it pays off significantly.

What we mean by reviewing is that your child goes over all of their material. Regardless of what it is, they need to engage with everything again. The process of reviewing needs to incorporate elements of speed and retrieval. It is up to you to get the necessary material from the teacher. Constant reviewing becomes easier and faster each time your child reviews, further solidifying the neural connections.

REVIEWING IS THE ONE THING WE ALL KNOW WE SHOULD DO, BUT DON'T DO.

Your child's brain is fast, so don't be afraid to let them study fast. They can accomplish more than you think in as little as five minutes. You don't want them to go so fast that they make mistakes, but neither do you want them to go so slow that they get bored or daydream. Have them go as quickly as they can. Let them skim through the material or bounce from subject to subject to keep their brain engaged.

We recommend scheduling an ERR (Engage, Retrieve, Repeat) program for your child. Here's a simple schedule for the week.

MON.	TUES.	WED.	THUR.	FRI.	SAT. + SUN.
STUDY: -MONDAY'S MATERIAL (*UNTIL YOU KNOW IT.)	REVIEW: -MONDAY STUDY: -TUESDAY'S MATERIAL *	REVIEW: -MONDAY -TUESDAY STUDY: -WEDNESDAY'S MATERIAL *	REVIEW: -MONDAY -TUESDAY -WEDNESDAY STUDY: -THURSDAY'S MATERIAL *	REVIEW: -MONDAY -TUESDAY -WEDNESDAY -THURSDAY STUDY: -FRIDAY'S MATERIAL *	↻ REVIEW THE WEEK'S MATERIAL QUICKLY

Fig. 4.5

After your child has reviewed a day's worth of material on five consecutive days, they don't have to be as aggressive in reviewing and can increase the period between sessions. For instance, your child could first go over their material daily, then weekly, and then monthly. Though this will take some extra time, you will be surprised how well your child will end up knowing the material. You might even see their view of learning transform. Once kids (and adults) get excited about learning and realize they *can* learn, it becomes fun and they want to learn. Their increased confidence and knowledge will propel them forward.

Not too long ago, a nine-year-old girl came for an office visit, and her face was beaming. She could barely contain herself before telling me that osteomyelitis is a rare bone infection. I had given her that word and had asked her to repeat it six times a day for three weeks, just like I do the red truck exercise. The pride and joy on her face (and her mother's face!) were exciting to see.

Interestingly, at the same time this little girl was in my office beaming, a high school student had also come in. However, he was complaining and being overly critical of his brain's ability, saying how hard school was and that he just couldn't do the work. But after he witnessed this girl's ability to recall osteomyelitis, he decided to give it a try. He soon experienced surprise at his own brain's ability and has now begun to confidently put his brain to work.

Information is not difficult; it's unfamiliar. Learning is the process of letting the unfamiliar become familiar. Once we understand that our children's brains are powerful, and we begin teaching them according to how they learn best, they will start to experience the joy of learning.

5. Memorize Like a Champion

Did you know that memorizing is considered a sport? There are competitions both nationally and internationally in which memorizers of all ages get together and—you guessed it—memorize. Individuals compete to learn as much as they can in as little time as possible. Alex Mullen recently broke the record for how fast one could memorize a deck of cards, succeeding in 16.96 seconds.

He also holds the record for memorizing an 1,100-digit number in 15 minutes. Another memory athlete recently memorized 34 decks of cards in an hour.[24] Wow!

What are we to make of such stunning abilities? Our first reaction is to think that these guys are in some category by themselves, and we conclude that their brains are different from ours. As it turns out, many memory champs often confess they were poor students and displayed no real gifts or strengths in school.

That should make our heads spin a bit. So how do we explain their success? Technique.

You have probably used memory strategies yourself. Maybe you remember the acronym "PEMDAS" or the mnemonic phrase "Please Excuse My Dear Aunt Sally" as a way of remembering the order of operations in math.

P	Parentheses
E	Exponents
M	Multiplication
D	Division
A	Addition
S	Subtraction

Memory champs use another technique, based on the same premise: to take something hard to remember and make it easy to remember. Without going into great detail, here's the gist. Turn numbers/words into pictures, and use those pictures to form a story. It's as simple as that. Your brain will do the rest.

The two primary methods that employ this technique are the *method of linking* and the *method of loci* (Latin for "locations"). In order to understand the value of this technique for your child, it's a good idea for you to experience it personally. Try the following exercises.

First, let's consider the *method of linking*, where you will be "linking" two images together through the use of a story. This works great for whenever you need to memorize random facts that don't require being recalled as part of a list or sequence.

Let's say, for example, you need to memorize that William Shakespeare wrote *Hamlet*. The first thing you need to do is turn each of these items into a picture that you can easily visualize. The more vivid and ridiculous, the better. So what could represent Shakespeare? How about a milkshake with a spear for a straw? And then what could represent *Hamlet*? How about a giant Thanksgiving ham? Can you see each of them in your mind's eye?

Once you have your images, all you need to do is "link" them together through the use of a story. Again, be as creative and ridiculous as you can, and put yourself in the story to make it more memorable. For example, imagine you are sitting down at Thanksgiving dinner and in the middle of the table is that huge *ham*. Just as everyone is about to eat, you jump up and pour the *milkshake* all over the *ham*!

At test time, if you are asked who wrote *Hamlet*, you remember the image you selected for *Hamlet*—the ham. Once you remember the *ham* you will immediately recall the story of the *milkshake with the spear* at Thanksgiving. You would then ask yourself, what does the *milkshake* represent? Shakespeare! To make things even more memorable, try incorporating other senses into your stories like taste, touch, smell, and hearing. It's a strange technique, but it works.

The *method of linking* does, however, have limitations. If you try to connect multiple items into a storyline, each image is entirely dependent upon the cue before it. If you forget one "link" in the chain, you may not be able to find the rest of the memories. This is why I do not recommend the *method of linking* for lists or anything that requires a sequence. But to quickly memorize facts, it's a great choice that requires little effort.

The next method to consider is the *method of loci*, or what is now commonly called the *memory palace technique*. This technique has been around for ages, and it's what all the great orators of the ancient world would have regularly used to recite their long, detailed speeches from memory. This might seem a little weird to you, but give it a shot, this is where the power and fun really begin!

Instead of linking images to each other, you are now going to link images to preexisting locations. Let's imagine you have a list of 10 items that you need to memorize. First, you have to set up your 10 locations where you will store the 10 items. You are going to store one item in each of the locations. For this example, let's choose 10 locations on your body. In order, they are your feet, knee, hip, belly button, chest, mouth, nose, eyes, forehead, and the top of your head. Go ahead and close your eyes, visualizing all 10 locations.

Your list of 10 items to memorize includes *bacon, marker, elephant, egg, phone, Frisbee, books, pepperoni pizzas, train*, and *orange juice*. Taking one at a time, you will combine or "link" the image with the locations you've already created. Remember to make your story as vivid and as ridiculous as you can. Make up your own stories or use the following examples. Go slow and try to really imagine and experience each story.

First, imagine wrapping a piece of *bacon* around your foot. Next, take a *marker* and draw a circle on your knee. Next, imagine an *elephant* suctioning your hip with his trunk. Next, imagine pulling an *egg* out of your belly button. Next, imagine your *phone* has been glued to your chest. Next, imagine catching a *Frisbee* in your mouth. Next, imagine blowing hundreds of *books* out of your nose. Next, imagine you have *pepperoni pizzas* as eyes.

Next, imagine a *train* zooming across your forehead. And finally, imagine pouring *orange juice* on top of your head.

Now it's time to test yourself. See if you can recall all 10 items. Start by first remembering each location. Visualize your feet. What else do you see? Do you see the *bacon*? Then visualize the knee. What else do you see? Continue in this manner through all 10 locations. How many can you get? My guess is that you can probably get all of them, or at least very close! Now, try reciting the list backward. Nice work!

If you are still with me, I have one more exercise for you. We started with the human body because it is an easy way for you to get the hang of the technique and to make the stories personal. Now we are going to translate the same technique to a different set of locations. Instead of using your body, we will use your kitchen. Starting clockwise from the doorway, make 10 locations (i.e. the fridge, dishwasher, sink, toaster, etc.). Make sure you can see and recall all 10 locations easily.

Then begin linking the 10-item list to your kitchen objects just like you have practiced. For example, you open the fridge and there's a *bacon* monster inside. You open the dishwasher and a giant blue *marker* has disintegrated inside it. The sink has an *elephant* in it and you are giving the *elephant* a bath. The toaster is shooting out *eggs*, and so forth. Continue making crazy stories for each item and location.

Once you have attached the 10 items to the 10 locations, try to close your eyes and mentally walk through the room, focusing on each location, and see how your brain marvelously recalls each item and story that you connected to that location. Pretty amazing, isn't it?

You can develop the *memory palace technique* with great freedom, adding extra rooms and objects. It's easy to then see how it's possible to memorize 10 rooms each with 10 items, giving you a total of 100 locations. You just have to set up your locations, but once you do, the memorizing is a breeze. This is the exact technique that memory champs use to accomplish their unbelievable feats.

If it is a little hard at first, stick with it. The technique is a skill just like any other skill. Over time you will get better at it. You may notice that sometimes items don't pop back into your memory when looking at the location. That is normal. Consider it a learning opportunity. Ask what went wrong in the linking. This is usually where the breakdown happens. Was the story vivid enough? Was it weird or crazy? Was there action in it? Did you incorporate other senses?

Once you have a basic grasp of the technique, try teaching it to your child. They can use this technique to memorize vocabulary, a list of facts about a particular subject, or to memorize points on an upcoming essay exam. To memorize numbers or dates, turn the number into an image that will cue the number. For example, a swan could represent the number two because it looks like a two, or car keys could represent the number sixteen because that's when you get your license.

The *memory palace technique* is fun to use, fosters creativity and imagination, produces a mental workout, and gives a serious boost to self-confidence. No child (or parent) can hold back a smile when they first experience their brain working on this level. I've done this with kids in my office. It blows everyone away. Disability? I don't think so.

WHY IT WORKS

First, the brain is weak at remembering abstract ideas and numbers, but it is incredibly strong at remembering images and stories that are concrete. That's why we may quickly forget someone's name but usually remember their face. The name is abstract while the face is more concrete. There's more data in a face than in a group of letters.

Secondly, the more brain energy that is used to understand something, the more memorable it becomes. When you create a story that is personal, involves all the senses, and is as vivid as possible, you are firing up the whole brain, deeply engaging both the left brain (analytical) and right brain (creative) hemispheres.

A third reason why the *method of loci* works so well is that our brains are particularly good at spatial memory. The *method of loci* builds upon spatial memory structures in the brain, which further allows for intangible, abstract ideas to become concrete in our thinking.

6. Cultivate Creative Play

Einstein went back to the basics; he studied time and space. Einstein was smart, but what made the difference for him was that he had the freedom to be creative and to look at things in a fresh way.

> **HELPING YOUR CHILD LEARN LIKE EINSTEIN IS ABOUT SUPPORTING THEIR PASSION AND GIVING THEM SPACE FOR CREATIVE EXPRESSION.**

How many times have we said about a new product on the market, "Why didn't I think of that?" We don't let our creative minds emerge; therefore, we don't allow ourselves to come up with what might seem to be a natural invention. The idea of gravity was seen as heresy when Isaac Newton first proposed it with the drop of an apple. The current establishment's creativity was blocked to accepting gravity, not because it wasn't right but because it wasn't the usual way of thinking.

Helping your child learn like Einstein is about supporting their passion and giving them space for creative expression. It's not about making them mindlessly learn facts. It's about opening their world through exploration, discovery, and imagination. Einstein once explained, "Imagination is more important than knowledge. Knowledge is limited. Imagination encircles the world."[25] Expect your child to learn facts taught in school but also encourage them to express their creativity, to dream, and to wonder. That is what play is all about.

As a member of the National Coalition of Play, I've learned a lot about the significant role of play in the development of learning skills. Often we think of play as the absence of learning, but we are beginning to understand that play may be the primary way we learn, especially for children. It's through playing that children develop cognitive, social, and creative skills. Some educators have built entire learning programs on the "learning by playing and playing to learn" paradigm. Dr. Hallowell attributes the cognitive benefits of play largely to the effect play has on developing the prefrontal cortex—boosting one's ability to organize, interpret, and respond to information effectively.

The act of playing also has benefits outside of cognitive development. When children play, they release stress, find enjoyment in the world, and connect with others. When play involves exercise, it increases their physical health. Therefore, it's important to take play very seriously!

Here are three tips to foster creative play for your child:

1. Create a Safe Environment

When fostering an environment for our kids to play and explore their creativity, they need to feel emotionally safe. An environment filled with the pressure of performance will short-circuit your child's creative process. Don't worry if the time *feels* wasted. If the child is engaged, it's not. Thomas Edison made 1,000 light bulbs before one worked. Our kids need to be able to play without feeling like they must perform—that's where real play happens, and that's the soil in which creativity blossoms.

Emotional safety also means allowing your child to be and become whomever they desire. If you ask a group of first and second graders who the artists are in the group, everyone raises their hand. If you ask a group of fourth graders the same question, only a handful of children might raise their hands.

What happened? Where did all the artists go? If you look at the fourth grader, you can note the inhibitions of play and their decrease in imagination, as fear of "exposure" and "not measuring up" becomes real to them. They become afraid to say or do the wrong thing, and that fear strips them of their creativity and passion. Who knows how many artists are out there who were never allowed the freedom to create? What would have happened to Leonardo da Vinci if he hadn't been adopted by a family that gave him the opportunity to explore his gifts?

Dr. Hallowell, in his book *Shine*, shares a story of how he personally observed a radical difference in play between two groups of chemistry students that were entering Harvard. The first group, upon arrival, jumped into the lab and began tinkering with everything they could get their hands on, solving problems and making new discoveries. The second group stood around waiting for instructions and actually feared the thought of being set loose in the lab.

What a difference! The first group was fully alive. They had been waiting for this moment for years. The second group had no ability to play, and for them, chemistry was about fulfilling duties and advancing their careers. Hallowell notes that they "may get the degree they seek, but they never make much of a difference in the field, and worse, they rarely take much joy in what they do."[26]

Creating a safe environment for your child is possibly the greatest thing you can do to help cultivate creative play. When a child is playing, they aren't conscious of what others are thinking about them. Playing is about being fully engaged and fully alive in the activity, what some call being "in the zone" or having "flow." When parents, teachers, coaches, or friends begin judging and criticizing, the child becomes self-conscious. And self-consciousness becomes the enemy of play because it causes the child to live in fear of trying to please others, measure up, or fulfill duties. Creating a safe environment is about letting your child's imagination run wild, explore uncharted territory, and make new connections in the world. It's about supporting them wherever their journey takes them without criticizing them or pressuring them to conform to your own expectations.

Play doesn't work like that. Put a bunch of rules or expectations on a child, and their play instinct dries up. Before long they are reduced to a chemistry student who has long forgotten the joy and wonder of playing in the lab.

2. Create an Intentional Environment

As a parent, creating a safe environment doesn't mean you are completely hands-off. The trick is to steer and guide your child while supporting their creativity and learning, not dominating them in the process. Imagine the way a vine grows up a trellis. Too much trellis suffocates the plant, and too little trellis doesn't allow for the plant to get off the ground. But with just the right amount of trellis, you support the plant's organic life and give it direction to grow.

In the same way, you are to provide guidance that fosters creativity and passion but not so much that it suffocates your child. You might bring out a bin of items, and those are the only items your child can play with for a given amount of time. Whether it's blocks or musical instruments, you have intentionally set a structure inside which their creativity can flow.

To illustrate the point, I once conducted a little experiment on my own. I took 20 ADHD kids of various ages and divided them into two groups of 10. Both groups had access to a box of items (soccer ball, tire, hula hoop, etc.), but my instructions for each group were different. For the first group, I gave them each an item and told them exactly what I wanted them to do with it. In the second group, I put the box of items on the ground and walked away. The results were fascinating. The first group failed to do what I told them to do and ended up bored and milling around. The second group unleashed their creative forces, and after 30 minutes, I had to pull them off the playground.

The first group of children illustrates that too much domination short-circuits creative play. But also notice that without further support, they became bored and idle. The second group had the right balance of structure and freedom, which caused their creative fire to ignite.

Joi Ito, director of MIT's Media Lab, builds their corporate philosophy on the belief that "education is something done to us, while learning is something we do for ourselves."[27] I couldn't agree more. Your job as a parent is to strike the careful balance of supporting your child's learning environment without overpowering it.

3. Shape the Environment around Your Child's Passions

You will produce more creativity in your child when you support their passions rather than force them to be interested in something else. Listen to your child. Know your child. If they love bugs, get outside and let them explore. Collect them and see if you can identify them, talking about their similarities and differences. It might be a science, or it could be the arts—music, dance, painting—or it could be a sport. You are trying to tap into the passion that makes your child come alive. Encouraging their interests alters their trajectory and gets them on a path to lifelong learning.

Remember, the subject matter is not what's most important; instead, it's the learning process, and the learning process can be applied to anything. Though the number of study skills abounds, we've intentionally given you our top six to implement. We are confident that as you begin, you and your child will be pleasantly surprised with the results. Let the learning journey begin!

SUMMARY

- Most of the fear and anxiety that parents experience revolve around their child's ability to learn and perform well in school.
- The FastBraiin mind is not at a disadvantage for learning, but it must be taught how to learn.
- If you want to help your child, teaching them to learn at home will provide the most significant outcomes.
- Establish an emotionally encouraging environment for your child.
- Set up a homework routine, and stick with it.
- Help your child bust through procrastination (pain) cycles by using the Pomodoro technique, music, and exercise and by focusing on the reward ahead.
- The FastBraiin study method for increased learning is a three-step process: engage, retrieve, and repeat (ERR).
- Utilize the *method of linking* and *method of loci* like the champs do to quickly and efficiently memorize facts and lists.

- Cultivate creative play with safe, intentional environments that tap into your child's passions.
- Support your child's passions.

CHAPTER 5

FLIPPING EDUCATION, PART II

How to Increase Learning at School

"Fighting to increase learning at school is an uphill battle, but it's a battle worth fighting and a battle you can win."

Implementing the right study skills and allowing for creative play are vital in fostering a conducive learning environment for your child. The other side of the coin is how to promote a similarly conducive environment at school. It's more difficult to influence learning at school because you have less control over your child's day. Each teacher is going to teach differently, and every year your child's teachers will change. Teachers will have varying degrees of awareness of ADHD and how to help those with learning and focusing issues. Teachers want to help each of their students learn, yet much of their day is spent controlling behavior. It is rare to find teachers who understand and are knowledgeable about ADHD children and how to help them focus, learn, and utilize their strengths. The entire education system, for that matter, is not conducive to working with FastBraiin children.

John Medina, PhD, Director of the Brain Center for Applied Learning Research at Seattle Pacific University and author of *Brain Rules*, emphatically states, "If you wanted to create an educational environment that was directly opposed to what the brain was good at doing, you would probably design something like a classroom."[28] And that's for all students, not just those with ADHD!

Fig. 5.0

It would be nice if we could rebuild the education system, but that's not where we find ourselves, at least not yet. Many parents do not have access to alternative schools (although they are becoming more popular). Therefore, we should make the best use of the system as it is. Fighting to increase learning at school is an uphill battle, but it's a battle worth fighting and a battle you can win.

Here are a few strategies that we have found to consistently increase learning at school:

1.   Establish a Relationship with Your Child's Teacher

Establishing a relationship with your child's teacher is critical. The goal should be to form a partnership between you and the teacher that mutually and cooperatively seeks to benefit your child. School is usually the first place parents learn that their child has an issue, and the teacher is most often the person who breaks that news. It's hard for parents to hear and accept that their child is disruptive or that they may have a learning disorder. Defenses go up, and in many cases, the teacher becomes a scapegoat. We might even think the teacher is "picking" on our child or doesn't like our child.

Parents must not vilify their child's teacher but instead accept what they say, ask a lot of questions, and express support for the teacher. Friction between you and the teacher will rarely benefit your child. Protecting and nourishing your relationship with the teacher protects and nourishes the teacher's relationship with your child. Being defensive and accusing the teacher hurts your child in the long run. Your child can pick up on the negative emotion between you and the teacher within the first month of the new school year. And that negativity will compound itself over time.

It's critical that your child believe that you and the teacher are on the same page and that you are working together. Make sure your child knows that you support the teacher's classroom policies and expectations. If you disagree with the teacher and need to address an issue, meet with the teacher privately. If you criticize the teacher in front of your child, you will cause unnecessary stress. You also undermine the needed respect for teachers, which only exacerbates your child's behavior and learning problems.

> # PROTECTING AND NOURISHING YOUR RELATIONSHIP WITH THE TEACHER PROTECTS AND NOURISHES THE TEACHER'S RELATIONSHIP WITH YOUR CHILD.

It may help for parents to remember that teachers have your child's best interests at heart. That's why they became teachers. You may not see eye to eye on everything, but hopefully, you share the same goal: to help your child learn and grow as a person. You don't have to give in to the teacher if you disagree, but try to see the situation from their perspective.

Teachers have your child in the classroom for more than six hours per day, which is more interaction time than you will have with them at home. They will see them in situations that you may never have an opportunity to witness. They see them interact with peers. They learn how they respond to pressure and performing. Because of their education, experience, and exposure to many children, most teachers know the age-appropriate behaviors as well as how children should be performing academically. If the teacher suggests that your child may have an issue, you need to understand that their concern is well-intentioned and comes from a knowledgeable place.

Be open-minded with what the teacher says. Listen well. You'd be foolish not to listen. But don't accept generalities. Instead, ask them for specific examples to help you better understand what's going on. Teachers, however, cannot diagnose and should not make the claim that a child has ADHD. Rather, they should tell you what they observe in the classroom and may suggest you talk with your doctor. If you decide to visit a doctor regarding your child's issue, keep in mind the differences in the settings. The doctor's office is a one-on-one setting in a quiet room. The classroom, however, is full of children and distractions. The behavior the doctor sees may be very different from what happens in the classroom, but that doesn't discount the truthfulness of what your child's teacher has observed.

Ask the teacher what you should be doing at home and in what areas your child needs extra help. Ask about strategies that you can implement at home that will help in the classroom. We utilize a FastBraiin form as well as the Vanderbilt form to assist the teacher in assessing your child. These types of forms can be beneficial for you and provide valuable information for your child's doctor.

Forming a partnership with the teacher is a give-and-take relationship. By listening to the teacher and asking questions, you will earn their respect, and they will be more open to listening to you. It is beneficial to share with the teacher about your child, to help them understand your child better, and to glean information that may be helpful in teaching them. The teacher should naturally be open to the discussion, but be careful not to be too demanding of the teacher, or they may feel threatened. It may be helpful to make a list each year of the things that have worked for your child and continue to update the list and develop it in collaboration with your child's future teachers.

If your doctor prescribes medicine for your child or if you are making a medication change, always begin at home over a weekend. The extra time at home will allow you the opportunity to see how the medicine is affecting your child, as you know them best. Let the teacher know when your child is taking medication or when they change their medication. The teacher is your friend and can help you navigate through a critical observational window of your child's medication response. If they are made aware, they can be proactive instead of reactive to inform you of any mood swings or behavior changes that might arise.

I recommend one final note on building the parent-teacher relationship. It's very important that you express gratitude to the teacher for their efforts to educate your child. That might be difficult, especially if you don't see eye to eye with them, but I challenge you to overcome that barrier. A kind and encouraging word may go a long way in empowering the teacher to help your child. Teachers need encouragement, regardless. They spend countless hours laboring over children and need to be appreciated for the work they do.

2. Advocate for Your Child

Your child has every right to be successful, and it is your job to expect that your child *will* be successful. Become familiar with available resources designed to help your child in the classroom. Ask your child's teacher. Talk with the school counselor or principal. Help is available; don't stop until you find it.

Typically, your child will go through the RTI (responsiveness to intervention) process when they are struggling in the classroom and fall below grade level. Schools across the United States use this process for both academic and behavioral issues. The RTI helps your child's teacher identify interventions that will improve your child's specific challenges. It will also help the teacher determine the amount of extra support your child needs weekly to be successful. Many children will improve with interventions. If your child continues to struggle with the maximum amount of added support (90 minutes/week), they may require professional testing to look more closely at learning disabilities, depression, IQ, and achievement tests that show weaknesses and strengths. This type of assessment will help the school determine whether specialized services are needed.

3. Take Advantage of an IEP and a 504 Plan

Two great legal resources in the school system are an IEP and a 504 plan. An individualized education plan (IEP) is a written legal document that describes how a school plans to meet your child's educational needs. A child must qualify for an IEP based on scores determined by psychological testing.

The 504 plan refers to Section 504 of the Rehabilitation Act and the Americans with Disabilities Act, which specifies that programs receiving federal funding may not exclude individuals with disabilities from participating. It entitles all children to a free and appropriate education and eliminates barriers that exclude children with disabilities.

What Is the Difference between an IEP and a 504 Plan?

An IEP adds services to foster equality (for example, it allows a student to receive reading instruction on a lower level). A 504 plan removes barriers in order to foster equality (for example, it allows a student to receive shorter assignments).

ADHD children don't necessarily need one of these levels of support, but it's important to discuss the RTI process with your child's teacher and understand the intervention services provided by the school.

Other factors play a role in a child's inability to meet prevailing standards in the classroom. It's important to pay attention to variables at home—such as diet, sleep, and exercise—that can be changed to benefit your child's focus at school.

Conferencing with your child's teacher is vital. Ask for meetings at regular intervals. Discuss what strategies work best for your child. Be open to listening to their feedback. Caring for your child is a team effort. Be careful not to quickly remove your child from their current classroom in order to put them into a special class. Sometimes this may aggravate the situation, instead of making things better. Try first to make things work with their current teacher in their current classroom. The importance of excellent communication between you and your child's teacher cannot be overemphasized.

Many children will raise their grades with the accommodation of an IEP or a 504 plan. Unfortunately, when this happens, schools have been known to withdraw their support, stating that the child no longer requires this assistance. But in December 2016, a law went into effect stating that the school system can no longer withdraw these services.

4. Encourage Positive Reinforcement at School

How many times have you heard that your child is not behaving as expected in class? Maybe the teacher has called or sent you an email. Maybe your child has come home feeling like the teacher doesn't like them because of discipline issues at school. Children with ADHD need a structured, nonchaotic classroom, where the expectations and routines are clear as well as predictable and consistent.

Positive reinforcement is always the best policy in the classroom, as it builds self-esteem and confidence in the child. The teacher should regularly affirm and praise children when they are doing something right. For example, the teacher can say,

"Anna, I like how your eyes are on me, showing me you are ready to listen" or "I am so proud of you, Steven, for all of the hard work you put into this assignment." Statements like these motivate the child, as well as the class, to want to demonstrate that particular behavior.

When talking with your child's teacher, you might mention that your child responds best and behaves best when spoken to in this manner. Explain what has worked in the past. The last thing you want to do is tell your child's teacher they are doing everything wrong. That won't get you anywhere. Start small.

5. Use a Behavior Chart

When students consistently have difficulty managing their behavior in the classroom, they may benefit from a chart to help them be more aware of their ongoing struggles. Meet with the teacher and talk through the behavioral strategies that work best for your child. Often ADHD children simply forget to follow the rules and need to be reminded . . . over and over.

One strategy we've found that works well is to approach your child's teacher with a behavior plan. Hopefully, they would be interested, since everyone wins when your child behaves better. Ask the teacher if your child can have a brightly colored chart on their desk that outlines three to five desired behaviors that you are working on (both at home and at school). Each targeted behavior gets a 30-minute time slot incremented throughout the day, which allows for better self-monitoring on the part of the child and greater focus toward success. If the child performs the desired behavior during the 30-minute block, ask the teacher to place a positive reward in the box (i.e., smiley face, star, or sticker). The chart should not be marked in any way if they have not mastered the behavior (i.e., the boxes remain empty so that only positive feedback appears).

TIME:	9–9:30	9:30–10	10–10:30	10:30–11	11–11:30	11:30–12
RAISE HAND TO SPEAK	🙂		🙂	🙂	🙂	🙂
KEEP HANDS TO YOURSELF	🙂	🙂		🙂	🙂	
STAY ON TASK	🙂	🙂	🙂		🙂	🙂

* FIVE 🙂's → 15 MINUTES OF EXTRA RECESS

Fig. 5.1

The child should be rewarded either midday or at the end of each day if they have earned the number of positive marks required. It is a good idea to start out requiring only a few positive marks and gradually increasing the number of positive scores necessary each day or week so that the child has success early on.

Once the child becomes a master of the three to five behaviors, add new ones to the chart. Rewards might be 10 minutes of video games at the end of the day, 5 minutes of extra recess, eating lunch with the teacher, or anything else that would be considered a reward to the child. No consequences or punishment should occur if the child does not meet the requirements for that day. They should be encouraged that although they put forth a great effort, they didn't earn a reward and will have another chance tomorrow. It's better to have your child aiming for reward rather than trying to avoid punishment. Keeping the focus on the positive will motivate the child to continue making an effort and will help build their self-esteem.

This system works best when there is consistent parent-teacher interaction. The stronger the relationship you have with the teacher, the more likely the teacher is going to be willing to engage in something like a behavior chart.

> # IT'S BETTER TO HAVE YOUR CHILD AIMING FOR REWARD THAN TRYING TO AVOID PUNISHMENT.

So start developing your relationship with the teacher early on. Inform the teacher about your child, about the behaviors you are working on at home, and about what strategies you have found to work. You want to be a source of encouragement to the teacher, not someone trying to dictate how they are to do their job. That will tear down your relationship rather than build it up, so be sensitive and thoughtful in your interactions. If it's too much of a burden for the teacher to record the child's behavior every 30 minutes, have the teacher do larger blocks like an hour, or just for the morning or afternoon. At the very least, you should be able to receive feedback on the entire day.

6. Overcome Test Anxiety

Anxiety can start at an early age. We do not treat anxiety with medication until a child is at least 8–10 years of age, and only if the anxiety is causing significant difficulty in the child's ability to function within their environment.

It's not uncommon for FastBraiin individuals to struggle with testing due to the anxiety they experience in the moment. Anxiety is the worry and fear that something terrible is going to happen. As we've discussed, anxiety causes a sequence of physiological responses to take place, which ultimately short-circuits the brain's ability to perform well—which creates more stress, and the vicious cycle has begun. A child becomes particularly frustrated when they know the answers to a test but fail to perform when it matters.

With a little practice, however, your child can learn to remain calm under testing pressure. Have your child . . .

- Practice deep breathing or relaxation techniques before and during the test. Try breathing in slowly for 10 seconds and breathing out for another 10 seconds.
- Develop good test-taking skills—break tests into smaller parts and work on the easier parts first to build confidence and ensure completion of those parts.
- Ask to take the test alone and not with the class.
- Ask the teacher to give them an oral test before or after school or during lunch.
- Try helping your child keep a positive thought in their mind, like the feeling of doing well, or perhaps even something unrelated to school, like dance class or playing with their dog.
- Get a good night's sleep.
- Exercise and eat healthy. Morning walks are great.
- Listen to music. If that's not possible, have your child hum quietly or sing in their head.
- Practice taking timed tests beginning three days before a test.

It's vital that you encourage your kids! Parents can address underlying fears that may be present with test-taking. Even subconsciously, a student may fear failure for a variety of reasons. There could be a fear of looking dumb to friends, of not getting into the best school, or of not meeting their parent's expectations.

It is essential that parents reinforce their unconditional support. Let your child know that their grades don't determine their worth. Let them know you believe in them and love them no matter what.

7. Prepare for School Success at Home

How you function at home also affects how your child will act and behave at school.

To prepare your home for classroom success—

- Establish a morning routine to minimize stressors and reduce morning mayhem. This routine will benefit you and your child. Make a list of the tasks your child must do to get ready for school. Print a copy of the checklist and encourage your child to follow it.
- Feed your child a healthy breakfast and pack a healthy lunch (high protein and healthy fats, low carbs—more on this later).
- Turn off the TV and video games in the morning, and turn them off two hours before bedtime.
- Determine an after-school routine that will help the evenings be productive and efficient.
- Have homework done and in book bag by the door before going to bed.
- Get a good night's sleep. Try to have your child go to bed at the same time every night. A typical child, age 6–10, needs around 10 hours of sleep each night. Some may require more.
- Use a timer to give the mornings a better flow. Place the timer on your child's bedside table and at the breakfast table, and if your child beats the timer getting out of bed and dressed or getting to breakfast, you can reward them.

Writing out goals and making a checklist will build independence in your child and diminish struggles that make everyone's blood pressure rise. A list helps begin everyone's day on the right foot. Develop a similar routine after school and at bedtime to keep evenings calm.

To promote a healthy view of home and school, we recommend not disciplining at home for what goes on at school. You should talk about it, but make sure you end the conversation on a positive note. If you've had a bad day at work, what do you want when you get home? Probably not to be chastised by your spouse and sent to bed without dinner. When you embrace your child and talk positively with your child about school, the home remains a refuge, and a positive view of school remains intact.

SUMMARY

- Influencing your child's education while at school is difficult, but you can still make a significant impact.
- Be an advocate for your child. Build a relationship with your child's teacher and ask about special programs and resources that may benefit your child.
- Without being too demanding, carefully share with your child's teacher what strategies have helped your child's learning and behavior at home. Encourage positive reinforcement.
- If your child struggles with testing, help them implement anxiety-reducing strategies before and during the test.
- School success begins at home with routines, good sleep, nutrition, exercise, limiting screen time, and of course, being positive.
- Poor behavior at school is disciplined at school—not at home where you should provide support. Talk about what happened at school, keep your emotions in check, and end with something positive.

CHAPTER 6

FLIPPING EXERCISE

How to Increase Performance through Movement

*"Until exercise becomes a part
of our learning strategy, we are
shortchanging our kids."*

We all like a good investment, right? If we could go back in time, we'd likely invest in Google, Apple, and Facebook. No question! We'd all be doing very well. When it comes to education, research is now telling us that what we should have been investing in all along is exercise, not the latest self-help book, study technique, or drug. But there's a massive disconnect. As research on the benefits of exercise grows, our kids are actually exercising less and less. It's time to wake up!

Dr. John Ratey, a Harvard University psychiatrist, in his book, *Spark: The Revolutionary New Science of Exercise and the Brain*, shows with compelling evidence that exercise is equal to or out-performs other strategies in addressing cognitive impairment, lack of focus, depression, anxiety, obesity, and an overall decline in health.[29] His evidence does not say that other measures are unnecessary, just that exercise deserves more credit than most professionals give it. If you want to make a sound investment in physical and mental health for your child, exercise is key.

We see this connection all the time in our clinics, and maybe you've had this experience yourself. While you are participating in a sport or athletic activity, everything else in life seems to get a little better. That's what happens to our athletes at the high school and college levels. They all tend to do better during the season of their sport than they do during the off-season, and improvement is across the board—in their mood, ability to concentrate, grades, and overall health.

In the face of a growing body of data supporting the benefits of exercise, our society chooses to exercise less and less. ADHD children, who are in constant need of moving around, get punished for their movement in the classroom by not being allowed to go to recess. That is just dumb!

Exercise releases energy and increases social and cognitive skills, including the ability to learn and perform well on tests. ADHD individuals tend to have "extra" energy and can mentally be all over the place; therefore, the lack of exercise makes it particularly difficult for them, more so than to non-ADHD individuals. Punishing them for being energetic by keeping them in from recess is the very opposite of what teachers should be doing to curb their problematic behavior.

RECESS SHOULD BE TREATED AS A CLASSROOM FOR LEARNING.

Keeping kids in from the playground happens not only in the name of punishment but also in the name of productivity—replacing playtime with more class time. Recess should be treated as a classroom for learning. We've bought into a false dichotomy that sees learning and exercise at odds with one another. Physical activity supports and influences the entire learning process—from acquisition and understanding to problem-solving, recall, and test-taking—as well as the physical growth and development of a child. We might think we've advanced in our education system by taking out recess, but overall grades are suffering.

Studies have shown that decreasing recess time (and increasing instructional learning time) has had an ironically counterproductive effect on grades. It is better fitness in children that is correlated with better grades.[30] Animal studies have shown that mice who exercised had twice the number of neurons in the learning and memory center of their brains than mice who didn't.[31]

Yet what has the education system done with this research? Not much. We are stuck in our old ways. With an increasing number of teachers favoring more academic rigor in place of recess (due to increasing EOG demands), the American Academy of Pediatrics found it necessary to release the following statement: "Recess is a crucial and necessary component of a child's development and, as such, it should not be withheld for punitive or academic reasons."[32] In the final analysis, it is counterproductive to withhold exercise for behavior management or academic benefit.

Although the education system has been slow to apply exercise science, the professional world has begun exploring this frontier, with personal coaches and leadership gurus incorporating exercise as a necessary component to increased productivity. "There is no question," exercise physiologist Jerome Zuckerman states, "that people who are fit are more productive, they enjoy their work more and accomplish more."[33] It's beginning to be a well-established norm within research and professional circles that productivity and enjoyment increase as exercise increases.

> # IT IS COUNTERPRODUCTIVE TO WITHHOLD EXERCISE FOR BEHAVIOR MANAGEMENT OR ACADEMIC BENEFIT.

Author of several books linking brain function to fitness, neuroscientist Chong Chen recently released a new research-driven book on exercise and its relationship to personal and professional productivity, arguing that exercise increases mental sharpness, boosts creativity, and helps people cope with stress, avoid burnout, and even beat jet lag.[34] Some corporations offer exercise programs for their employees, which not only take care of their employees but also boost the company's bottom line. Even some countries, like Japan, have introduced "exercise break" programs into their work culture with well-documented success.[35]

If top businesses in cutthroat environments and, in some cases, entire countries are taking exercise this seriously (where productivity is one of the primary goals), it's time for the education system to do likewise. Until exercise becomes a part of our learning strategy, we are shortchanging our kids.

Although exercising produces a broad spectrum of benefits, the three most critical benefits for the ADHD child are that exercise *improves focus and learning, improves mood, and decreases impulsivity.*

EXERCISE IMPROVES FOCUS AND LEARNING

"Exercise," Dr. Ratey argues, "provides an unparalleled stimulus, creating an environment in which the brain is ready, willing, and able to learn."[36] All this is largely due to the fact that exercise increases the amount of blood in the brain, something that may be of particular importance to ADHD individuals. Evidence suggests that most people with ADHD have below-average blood flow within their brain, which negatively affects their cognitive functioning. Exercise, therefore, directly counters this weakness by expanding blood vessels and increasing blood flow. When your child exercises, their brain cells immediately start functioning at a higher level, causing them to be more alert, awake, and focused.[37] That's why we suggest students exercise before studying, every 20 minutes during their study session, and just before taking a test.

BRAIN AFTER SITTING QUIETLY

BRAIN AFTER 20 MINUTE WALK

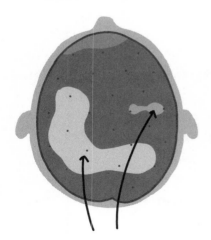
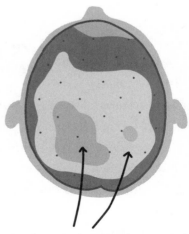

LIGHT GRAY AREAS DENOTE INCREASE

Fig. 6.0

Researchers have discovered a protein called brain-derived neurotrophic factor (BDNF), which is responsible for maintaining the health of neurons as well as establishing new neurons. What's fascinating is that BDNF levels in the brain spike during exercise. Although the exact reason for why this happens is still unclear, there's no question about the link between exercise and BDNF. Ratey likens BDNF to "Miracle-Gro" for your brain—it is fertilizer for neural activity. BDNF binds to neurons and increases their signal strength, allowing for improved communication between neurons. Interestingly, the presence of BDNF encourages more BDNF production as well as serotonin, our feel-good neurotransmitter, which also ramps up learning potential.

Therefore, a brain flooded with the Miracle-Gro of BDNF is ripe for focus, creativity, learning, and problem-solving. Ratey goes so far as to encourage us to even "think of exercise as medication."[38] Though I'm not advocating for anyone to stop medication without their provider's guidance, exercise certainly must be a necessary component to any plan of care.

Another benefit of exercise that directly promotes learning and productivity is its influence on executive function—the brain's CEO—the part of the brain responsible for processing, organizing, and responding to information. Exercise increases executive function, allowing us to zoom out of the details of our environment and see the "big picture." Individuals that aren't physically fit have a greater tendency to get lost in the details that make up larger systems. They can't put the pieces together.

Dr. Ratey's classic case study, which bears this research out in a real-world context, took place at a high school in Naperville, Illinois. Students who were struggling academically were offered the option of exercising before their hardest subject, to see if any difference was made on their grades. In the six years of the program's existence, on average the students that signed up for the exercise program read a half a year ahead of those who didn't, and in math, they performed more than two to four times better than their peers.

Paul Zientarski, coordinator of physical education at the high school, says, "People are dropping P.E. because test scores are failing. That's not the approach. That's the exact opposite of what you need to do to be successful."[39] The entire school, however, is encouraged to exercise. Kids are given heart rate monitors, taught about the brain benefits of exercise, and have access to a variety of fitness equipment. The school boasts some of the highest grades in the state, which Zientarski credits to their fitness-based education model.[40] And even more surprising, their eighth graders took the TIMMS test (Trends in International Mathematics and Science Study), competing against 230,000 other students around the globe, and finished first in science and sixth in math.[41]

EXERCISE INCREASES EXECUTIVE FUNCTION, ALLOWING US TO SEE THE "BIG PICTURE."

Well-performing executive function allows the brain to more quickly process information and organize that information into larger systems. It does this using fewer brain resources, making the brain more efficient. The executive function of the brain is also responsible for determining what is relevant or irrelevant at a given time. Stimuli that would typically be distracting to the individual have less perceived value. That's huge for the ADHD brain! It's vital, therefore, that individuals who may suffer from poor executive functioning make exercise a part of their daily routine.

EXERCISE IMPROVES MOOD

ADHD and depression often go hand in hand, and exercise helps counter these tendencies by releasing our "feel good" neurotransmitters. A positive mood translates into increased learning potential and productivity. Exercise also has the effect of increasing one's ability to control being irritable. Here at FastBraiin, we often utilize a brief exercise time when a child begins to feel irritable, anxious, or depressed.

Read any book on running, and it will most likely discuss the runner's "high." People who exercise regularly understand the positive emotions and feelings of well-being that occur after exercise. Duke University, not too long ago, performed their own study on Zoloft, a well-known antidepressant, comparing it to exercise. Their findings, published in *The New York Times* (although buried on page 14 of the health section) stated that Zoloft had no statistical advantage over exercise in treating depression. What's even more revealing are the results of a follow-up examination 10 months after the study. Only 8% of the exercise group fell back into depression. Compare that to 38% of those in the drug only group and 31% of those in the combined exercise and drug group that saw their depression return.[42] Ratey, therefore, argues that exercise is the best form of long-term, effective care for depressed people, contending that "[exercise] counteracts depression at almost every level."[43] To understand why, he says depression is largely a failure of neural connectivity, and exercise, he argues, is what "reestablishes those connections."[44] Exercise refreshes our brain and makes us feel better mentally and physically. A walk around the block in the evening improves our ability to fall asleep. Walking with family members is also a great time to catch up, communicate, and build relationships. All of this works to elevate mood. If your child is on medication or their medication is wearing off, they may become frustrated with schoolwork or studying at home or getting along with others. A brief run around the block or the house will result in a positive change. A burst of exercise increases the heart rate, breathing rate, and stimulates the brain to have a sense of well-being. A positive mood enhances one's creativity and ability to perform.

> # WHEN SOMEONE EXERCISES, THEY ARE MORE LIKELY TO INTERPRET AN EVENT AS POSITIVE RATHER THAN NEGATIVE.

Recently, I was watching a professional golf tournament, and the announcer commented, "It is hard for either of them to get going, as neither are playing good golf today!" They were both stuck in a cycle of negativity. A negative event leads to a negative thought and negative mood, compounding the problem, making another negative event more likely. The cycle can be hard to break, but this is where exercise has the remarkable ability to step in and turn things around. Exercise inserts positive emotion into the equation, resulting in positive thoughts and the likelihood of a positive event.

Often our positive and negative thoughts are the result of our interpretation of an event. There may be no objective value to an event, but we assign it a value through our interpretation. Two golfers may hit the same "bad" shot; one may interpret it as his life falling apart, and the other may interpret it as a learning opportunity. One interprets it negatively, the other positively. Who do you think will have a better chance of making the better second shot?

The player with the positive emotion will also be more creative in problem-solving. Try being creative when you are frustrated at work or upset with someone. It is very difficult!

When someone exercises, they are more likely to interpret an event in a positive rather than negative manner. Part of this may be due to how exercise helps us deal with stress. Research indicates that when someone is fit and exercises, their physical and psychological response to anxiety and stress improves. Exercise builds up a resilience so that events are not as threatening to us. And when coupled with a healthy diet, physical activity may provide considerable gains in executive function, the release of stress, and the regulation of mood.

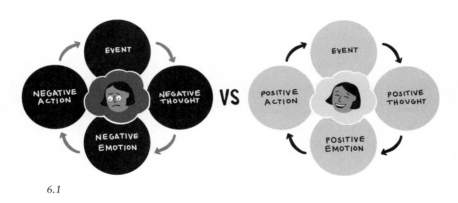

6.1

FastBraiin individuals appear to have more stress than the average child because they tend to worry more about performing and being accepted at home and among peers. It's a stress that invades every part of their lives. They have the sense that they are not as good or as smart as others. They worry about grades, falling behind, and getting into trouble. Stress, if appropriately managed, can be a good thing and inspire growth and productivity, but stress for most ADHD kids can be debilitating.

Exercise counteracts stress directly by leading children into positive emotional cycles instead of allowing them to flounder in negativity. Though there is an immediate boost in mood, exercise also produces long-term benefits by creating positive attitudes and habits.

EXERCISE DECREASES IMPULSIVITY

FastBraiin kids have been considered to have batteries bigger than their bodies.[45] Their relentless energy makes all of us sluggish adults jealous. If only we had half of their energy! Their batteries, however, get them into trouble when it's time to calm down. Our first educators designed the traditional classroom in opposition to FastBraiin kids who seem to have unlimited energy. Fidgeting has since become a typical symptom for diagnosing ADHD, as many children have serious difficulty sitting still. Exercise addresses this very issue by giving an immediate outlet for their energy. Their energy is not limitless. It's just pent up, and it needs to be spent. When children never have the opportunity to expend their energy, they become restless and impulsive. Therefore, the least corrective disciplinary action that teachers can take is to keep FastBraiin kids from recess as a form of punishment. The last thing these kids need is to be restrained from the playground where they can expend energy.

> # EXERCISE GIVES CHILDREN A GREATER ABILITY TO UNDERSTAND AND RESPOND APPROPRIATELY TO THEIR ENVIRONMENT.

The good feelings produced by exercise play a vital role. Your child's impulsivity may be their attempt to get an immediate pleasure. Sitting still and paying attention to their teacher profits little, while talking to other kids and making paper airplanes provide an immediate sense of pleasure. Exercise puts them in a feel-good state of mind and minimizes their desire to chase other sources of reward.

Exercise is not optional for ADHD individuals—it must become a part of their daily rhythm. When examining the wealth of benefits from exercise, we would be crazy not to intentionally weave it into their lives (and ours!). In *Brain Rules*, Dr. Medina summarizes his research by noting that children who have been active "are less likely to be disruptive in terms of their classroom behavior, . . . [they] feel better about themselves, have better self-esteem, have less depression, and less anxiety."[46]

We've primarily focused on three critical benefits of exercise—*it improves focus and learning, improves mood, and decreases impulsivity*—but there are several other substantial benefits as well. Exercise has been shown to promote restful sleep, improve digestion, strengthen immunity, provide structure and discipline, and develop critical social skills.

> # EXERCISE IS NOT OPTIONAL FOR ADHD INDIVIDUALS— IT MUST BECOME A PART OF THEIR DAILY RHYTHM.

This is quite a list. If there was a pill, or a medication, that could do all of this with no side effects, pharmaceutical companies would be pushing it like crazy, and I imagine the cost would be significant. People are already paying close to $10 a pill for their ADHD medication. The beautiful thing about exercise is that it's free, side effect free, 100% healthy and natural, and produces the same, if not better, long-term results as medication. As parents, we need to understand how incredible exercise can be for our kids. Let's replace hours of video games with exercise and play!

WHAT TYPE OF EXERCISE IS BEST?

If we know that exercise produces such wonderful benefits, we must then ask, What type of exercise is best? Exercise is the "exertion of physical energy" and can take place in a wide variety of activities. It may be structured, as in a workout program, or unstructured, as in recess on the playground. It might range from organized team sports like baseball to creative activities like dance. It can be serious, or it can be playful. Exercise takes many forms.

Although there is no hard-and-fast rule as to what type of exercise is best, there are some general guidelines to follow. The aim of exercise for the ADHD individual is to increase the heart rate and keep it raised for a duration of time. Cardio-intense exercise is the best type for the ADHD brain. Work the heart and get the blood pumping. Look for simple signs of heavy breathing and sweat. It's essential to monitor the type of exercise and its relationship with the desired outcome for your child. Dr. Ratey points out, "If exercise isn't showing the desired behaviors . . . the level of frequency, time exercising, and/or level of intensity needs to increase."[47] Tweak your child's program until you notice improvement in focus and behavior.

It's not all about the intensity, however. Exercise that your child enjoys will have a more significant long-term impact than exercise they see as drudgery. What sports or activities make your child come alive? Encourage your child in those areas and figure out how to incorporate these activities throughout the week. Soccer and lacrosse have taken off, as have the after-school martial arts programs. If your child has an interest in a specific sport or activity, help them get involved.

Also, consider exercises that involve constant motion, which are sometimes called chaos sports. ADHD children are especially good at these sports because they require continuous adaptation and spontaneity, which keep their brains maximally engaged. ADHD kids are not good at waiting. A game like baseball, with long periods of standing still or sitting, may not be as engaging or beneficial as a sport like soccer, which has a far greater impact on their cardio level.

In addition to sports and activities, there are plenty of excellent cardio exercises, such as jumping jacks, standing or jumping squats, jumping rope, push-ups, or even running in place. You might incorporate physical activity on a regular basis as part of your child's morning routine, starting the day with jumping jacks. Study breaks are a perfect time to boost the heart rate. Have your child shoot some hoops or jump rope between study sessions.

HOW LONG SHOULD MY CHILD EXERCISE?

Every individual is unique, so exercise demands may fluctuate depending on each child's specific makeup and the desired goals. However, I recommend 30 minutes of moderate to intense exercise daily. It is fine if your child does more than 30 minutes. I also recommend that the 30 minutes of exercise occur in one block of time, as opposed to doing six sessions of 5 minutes each. Your child's heart rate needs to remain elevated for longer than 5 minutes. If your child cannot achieve the more extended block of time, smaller increments of exercise are still better than none.

Research has shown that there are significant benefits of interval training (short bursts of high-intensity effort followed by rest). One such program that is incredibly efficient is Sprint8.[48] The essential protocol is to have your child go as fast and as hard as they can, doing jumping jacks, sprinting, and so on for 30 seconds followed by a 90-second rest period. Then repeat for a total of eight sessions. If you include a warm up and cool down of 2 minutes each (important to help prevent injury), the total workout time is only 20 minutes. Since interval training is so demanding, 20 minutes is a good stopping point. Otherwise, if you are doing more traditional forms of exercise, continue to aim for a session duration of 30 minutes.

Finding an Effective Activity Plan: Johnny's Story

When I saw 10-year-old Johnny for the first time, he was overweight and frustrated in school. When we talked about what he did for exercise, his mom was quick to say that she took him to soccer practice once a week and to his game once a week. She was thinking this was enough, while I was thinking to myself, "We have lots of work to do here—changes in exercise, diet, and study skills."

We started small, coming up with a daily activity chart in which Johnny did some form of exercise for at least 30 minutes a day. Included in this was exercising 5 minutes after every 20 minutes of studying. We also discussed the importance of nutritious meals and snacks and went over several study-skill strategies.

Slowly but surely, Johnny's weight dropped, and his grades improved. When I saw him at the office several months later, he told me, "Dr. Jim, I feel so much better!" I praised him for losing weight, getting his grades up, and following through with the plan we had established.

His mother shared that the whole family had become more active together, plus they were all eating better. Her words warmed my heart. "These changes have helped our family and deepened our relationships. Thank you!"

SIX HELPFUL TIPS TO GET YOUR CHILD MOVING

Regardless of your child's struggle to get in shape and stay active, they can find success with the right plan. Up to this point, we've discussed the significance of exercise, what it is, and how it benefits your child. You might be in complete agreement, but maybe you are like many parents and find it hard to bridge the chasm between knowing exercise is good for your kids and getting them to exercise.

1.   Any Exercise Is Better than No Exercise

Sometimes the hardest part is getting started. If jumping into a full-scale exercise program overwhelms you or your child, start small. Start with doing something that gets your child moving. Anything. They don't even have to know it's "exercise." They just need to get moving.

Many adults don't start an exercise program because they don't believe they have sufficient time. The same is true for how we view our children exercising. You may be surprised at what just five minutes of exercise can do, especially five minutes of activity done at different points during the day. It's also important to note that exercise is not just about the time it takes to exercise. It's also about the time it gives you back. Think about all the time that gets wasted when the brain is not at peak performance. Exercise produces a more efficient and capable brain, allowing for an increase in productivity, which at the end of the day means more time, not less.

Try encouraging your child to do 5 to 10 minutes of exercise first thing in the morning. Just a few minutes spent doing jumping jacks, running in place, and some stretching can benefit the body and mind. Five minutes here and there can help recharge and refocus the brain and over time can improve their overall health. Look for these little time gaps in which to incorporate exercise. Transitions between activities and during study breaks are perfect places for a quick exercise session. Johnson & Johnson has a powerful 7-minute workout online for free, and it comes with an app (great for adults too).[49]

> # YOU MAY BE SURPRISED AT WHAT JUST FIVE MINUTES OF EXERCISE CAN DO.

Kids are usually pretty good at exercise, but they need guidance. Give them a playground, and they play. Don't think that exercise has to look like a hardcore CrossFit workout. Running around with friends on the playground or in the backyard is great!

Keep a daily and weekly chart of the times and modes of exercise for your child. It may be helpful to share the chart with them and to bring them into the process. You can also give rewards for different goals along the way to keep up their motivation.

2. Aim for Consistency over Duration

It is better if you can get your child to do moderate exercise for even 15 minutes a day than to do an extended session once a week. A Saturday soccer game, for example, does not equal a week's worth of exercise.

Start slow and steady and focus on consistency. Once you have the consistency down, then start experimenting by adding more and more intensity and time as your child's body adapts to the changes. Keeping a schedule will help with consistency.

3. Try a Sport

Most sports are particularly beneficial for ADHD children. Participating in a sport gets your child moving without them feeling like they are exercising. The goal gets transferred from exercising to the objective of the sport, whether it's shooting the ball in the hoop or completing a full dance routine. Though the physical, mental, and social benefits of sports abound, sports are especially good at simply getting your child moving.

4. Set Tangible and Achievable Goals

The idea here is to set a goal and make it something that your child can attain. If your child hasn't been exercising, don't start off forcing them into an intense regimen. Instead, begin with a goal of 5–10 minutes a day for a week. Once they achieve this, continue to build on their progress. By setting achievable goals, you are increasing the likelihood that you and your child will stick with the plan. As they complete their goals, confidence grows, and the value of the plan gets reinforced.

5. Have Fun

Tapping into an exercise that your child finds fun has significant advantages. ADHD children can get bored quickly, but they don't get bored with what they enjoy. It's your job as a parent to find what they love doing and to figure out how to make exercise out of it.

Don't be afraid to change your exercise regimen or activities.

Keep things fresh and varied, and this will continue to engage their brain and add to the fun. Let them mix up their activities. Seasonal sports can be great for adding variety. Consider activities like biking, rollerblading, or hiking. There are a host of activities your child may find engaging and fun. And remember the playground, which is always a good option. You might even try bringing your child along with you when you exercise.

6. Don't Make Performance the End Goal

Another critical aspect of incorporating exercise into your child's life is to make sure that the focus of exercise does not become their performance. The end goal is not about winning prizes, losing weight, or getting a scholarship. Goals can be helpful, and it's fun to win, but you must always be careful that your child does not internalize winning or losing as their measure of worth.

Your child should know they are loved whether they win or lose. Instead of putting all the attention on your child becoming the next LeBron James or Mia Hamm, focus on developing their skills as a player or use sports as the "playing field" where you discuss valuable life lessons. If you lose focus of the bigger picture of your child's development, everyone loses.

> # YOUR CHILD SHOULD KNOW THEY ARE LOVED WHETHER THEY WIN OR LOSE.

For those of us with ADHD, staying physically active is not optional. Exercising can make the difference between being a D/F student and being an A/B honor roll student. A good exercise plan can change a student from one who struggles to focus into one who enjoys school and learning. To make the difference in your child's life, be sure to include physical activity as part of the over-all formula for optimizing their FastBraiin.

SUMMARY

- Exercise promotes mental and physical well-being for FastBraiin individuals by improving focus and learning, improving mood, and decreasing impulsivity.
- The best exercise for those with FastBraiin is cardio-intense, heart-rate-boosting exercise.
- We recommend a minimum of 30 minutes of daily exercise along with short bursts of exercise between study sessions at home.
- To help your child begin exercising regularly, set achievable goals, engage their passions, and aim for overall consistency.
- Exercising with your child is a great way to motivate them to exercise while also building your relationship.
- Keep exercise fun, and don't make performance the goal—for your child or for yourself!

CHAPTER 7

FLIPPING REST

How to Do More by Doing Less

"When it comes to the challenges facing children today, and especially FastBraiin kids, sleep may be the 'sleeping giant' that no one is paying attention to."

Have you ever heard a musician play hundreds of notes without taking a break? Listening to it can be uncomfortable and exhausting. When notes cascade on top of each other, it's noise rather than music. Music requires moments of sound followed by moments of silence. Both are necessary. Miles Davis, the famous trumpet player, once remarked, "It's not the notes you play, it's the notes you don't play." Good music requires alternating between activity and rest. Successful ADHD management is no different.

Those with FastBraiin are known for their constant zing, their relentless energy, and their go-go-go mentality, and these are some of their most significant assets. Trouble arises when they don't know how to slow down, don't know how to take a break, and don't know how to rest.

Rest is the counterbalance to activity and the catalyst to giving energy and purpose to your child's actions. In this chapter, we will focus on the importance of rest and how you can develop better resting habits for your child.

When thinking about rest, we must consider physical and mental rest. Though there is overlap between the two, both are critical. Physical rest takes place in the body during periods of calm, relaxation, and sleep. Mental rest takes place when the mind is at peace, thoughts are stable and clear, and there's an overall sense of well-being. It's critical that children (and adults) experience both types of rest. Overactivity without rest in either category is enough to send the ADHD individual into a tailspin.

Physical and Mental Rest

Many people ask, "What's the best way to start off the day?" The secret to getting a good day's start has little to do with the morning and has everything to do with the night before. One of the most reliable correlations to success is a good night's sleep. I know this may sound a bit anticlimactic, but this should be good news. It means that with a little bit of adjustment, you can make a significant impact on your child's growth and development.

REST IS THE COUNTERBALANCE TO ACTIVITY AND THE CATALYST TO GIVING ENERGY AND PURPOSE TO YOUR CHILD'S ACTIONS.

Although there is still some mystery about what sleep does for the body, there's no guesswork when it comes to whether or not sleep is essential. You know this yourself. How well do you perform after staying up until the early hours of the morning? How about when you wake up a couple of times during the night or even wake up an hour earlier? Your performance the next day will most likely suffer.

And how about your mood and your relationships? Are you as happy and focused on others, or are you a little more on the cranky and self-focused side? I'd expect the latter, which is our natural tendency when we are sleep deprived. We simply do not function well on less than optimal sleep.

But it's not all about productivity. If humans decrease the amount of sleep they get, serious health problems begin to surface. Sleep deprivation can play itself out in several alarming ways, including obesity, impaired cognitive function, behavior problems, increased inattention, progressive psychopathology, weak emotional regulation, cardiac disorders, immune disorders, accidental injury, and an increase of risky behavior and substance abuse.

The reason these issues arise is that sleep is the body's way of recharging and refueling as well as growing and developing. When sleep suffers, the body and brain suffer. Even the most basic human functions and processes demand good sleep.

Our "always on" culture presents a serious obstacle to getting better sleep. Over the last 50 years, we have seen a steady climb in the number of children and adults who could be considered sleep deprived. Today's children sleep, on average, one less hour per day than they did 50 years ago; that's 365 hours of less sleep per year. How are we to make sense of such a shift?

WHEN SLEEP SUFFERS, THE BODY AND BRAIN SUFFER.

Though a host of variables are likely responsible, consider the advent of modern technology; 24/7 access to entertainment, phones, and tablets; early school start times; late-evening activities; an increase in academic pressure; and an increase in parents working outside the typical nine-to-five schedule.

As a parent of a FastBraiin child, you have to take your child's sleep seriously. The FastBraiin individual is wired to be wired. And no, there's not a switch that can be flipped at 8:00 p.m. to turn your child's brain off and get them ready for bed. Their mind is always racing, and this makes going to sleep and staying asleep more difficult than it is for other kids. Until we become intentional about increasing their sleep, we can't get too upset when their behavior is out of control and they're having trouble learning.

When it comes to the challenges facing children today, and especially FastBraiin kids, sleep may be the "sleeping giant" that no one is paying attention to. It's time we address it. Dr. Sandra Kooij, founder and chair of the European Network Adult ADHD, argues that lack of sleep may be the cause of ADHD, not simply an effect of the condition. "There is extensive research showing that people with ADHD also tend to exhibit sleep problems," she says. "What we are doing here is taking this association to the next logical step: pulling all the work together that leads us to say that, based on existing evidence, it looks very much like ADHD and circadian problems are intertwined in the majority of patients."[50]

Why do we sleep? Robert Stickgold, an Associate Professor of Psychiatry at Harvard Medical School and one of the leading researchers on sleep, suggests that when we sleep, we process the day's activities, what we learned, and our emotional experiences.[51] Sleep improves our body's ability to grow and heal. During sleep, the brain washes away cell debris and releases growth hormone.

Getting enough sleep also improves our self-control. In the book *Peak Performance*, Steve Magness discusses the sleep study performed on the Stanford men's basketball team in 2011. Following an extra 1 hour and 50 minutes of sleep, those in the study improved their shots by 9%, sprints by 4%, and significantly improved their reaction time. He went on to discuss how NASA scientists found that with a 25-minute nap during the day, their "judgment was improved by 35% and vigilance by 16%."[52] And to my surprise, when compared to coffee, napping was better!

We also understand that getting kids to bed is no cakewalk. Here are four strategies that can increase your child's physical and mental rest.

1. Schedule Your Child's Sleep Routine

FastBraiin individuals need a plan for better sleep, or it won't happen. The common saying—"If you fail to plan, you plan to fail"—couldn't be more accurate when it comes to developing good sleep habits. It's too easy for other factors to keep your child awake.

Building a sleep routine begins with deciding on a bedtime. As much as possible, your child needs to go to bed at the same time every night. You may also try developing a pre-sleep ritual with your child, which will help cue the body and mind that it is time to get ready for sleep. To help your child wind down, consider including activities such as reading books, playing board games, or having a conversation about the day.

A typical school-aged child between the ages of 6 and 10 needs close to 10 hours of sleep each night. Keep in mind that some children require more sleep and some less. Regardless, try to make sure that all of their sleep occurs during the night—not by incorporating naps. Naps throw off the circadian rhythm sleep cycle.

There will be times when you and your child won't be in bed by your planned bedtime. That's normal, and that's okay. The point is to make sure that late nights are exceptions to the rule, not the norm. Going to bed and getting up on a regular schedule teaches your child's mind when to shut off and when to turn on.

2. Turn Off Screens at Night

Scheduling sleep sounds nice, but what if your child still has trouble falling asleep? It may be that they are not correctly preparing for sleep. Doing anything right requires proper preparation, and sleep is no different.

One of the primary ways to prepare your child for a good night's sleep is to have them avoid screen time before going to bed. Have you ever been lying down and sense that your eyes are in high gear, or perhaps you still see images of a screen when you're trying to sleep? Screens have a serious impact on our brains and on our sleep cycles.

The sleep cycle (circadian rhythm) sets the human body's rhythm and helps control the process of setting hormonal balances within the body. It involves sunlight and overall sleep time. The sun is the primary means by which the circadian rhythms get established for humans, and especially for children. However, the circadian rhythm can artificially be altered by the blue light coming from a computer, iPhone, or tablet screen. The blue light is so intense that it will cause the body to stop producing melatonin (a hormone that helps you fall asleep).

Blue light + FastBraiin mind = Problems falling asleep!

This also applies to us as parents and adults, which means it's not a good thing to be working on our computers or texting prior to going to bed.

> # GOING TO BED AND GETTING UP ON A REGULAR SCHEDULE TEACHES YOUR CHILD'S MIND WHEN TO SHUT OFF AND WHEN TO TURN ON.

We go to sleep when it gets dark not because we all got together and voted that 10 p.m. should be our bedtime but because melatonin is flooding our brain. When the sun shines, melatonin is turned off. When light from a tablet hits our retina, melatonin is turned off, signaling to the brain that it's time to be awake.

Any screen will do this, and studies indicate that glancing at a screen at night can disrupt melatonin production for up to four hours. Therefore, we recommend no screen time at least two hours before bedtime for adults and three to four hours before bedtime for children. As a parent of a child with FastBraiin, it's your responsibility to educate your child about the blue light and to enforce boundaries with screen time, and that includes all screens (tablets, phones, and computers), not just the television.

It's important to lead by example. Your children are watching you, and their screen habits will be influenced by your screen habits. At night, consider limiting your screen time. Instead, use this time to begin a longer pre-sleep routine and build the relationship with your child. Spend the time together reading a book or playing quiet games. This will not only prepare your child for sleep but will also provide them with many developmental benefits.

Limiting screen time is difficult with the digital revolution taking off as it has. We are more connected to our screened devices than ever before. Most people have a personal device of some sort and are able to access it at a moment's notice. If you as a parent do not set screen-time boundaries, your child will naturally engage in more and more screen time, as this is where our culture is headed—more people are now streaming movies and television shows than watching network TV.

The pressure to put screens in front of kids is exceptionally high. You're exhausted, the day has been long, the house is a mess, and the kids are loud and demanding. How tempting is it to put a screen in front of your child in order to catch your breath?

We know the challenge is real, and we aren't making light of it. That said, if you are going to help your FastBraiin child with their sleep patterns, you can't give in to screen time, no matter how tempting it may be; it's not helping your child or the family in the long run.

Your child will also likely put up a fight because they love their screen, and it has become a part of their routine. Older kids use screens to connect socially. Teenagers might text more than 100 times during the night. Having them give up screen time (including texting) is a challenge. It will certainly help if you lead by example.

Not only does your child need to quiet down, but the home needs to quiet down as well. When you can get the home environment under control, you will see your child begin responding appropriately. It won't work to tell your child to calm down and go to sleep when a TV is on in their room.

What I often hear from parents is that they calm down the house but allow their children to play on their iPads or computers just before bedtime. The house may feel calmer since no one is loud, but parents are putting their children's minds into high gear.

YOU CAN'T GIVE IN TO SCREEN TIME, NO MATTER HOW TEMPTING IT MAY BE.

The fallout is lack of deep sleep, which translates to a moody next morning and poor performance at school. Screen time before bed is not something to take lightly. We advise that there be no screens in the bedroom and no screens after dinner—that gets us closer to the rule of no screens three or four hours before bedtime.

We realize these recommendations may require changes, but the reward is worth the effort. It's not uncommon for us to hear from parents that the simple adjustment of removing screens in the evening had profound effects on the entire family, from deepening relationships to decreasing bedtime battles.

If your child needs to look at screens late (for something like homework), take advantage of recent advancements in technology that can automatically shift the color temperature of your screen based on the time of day. Many phones have this built in, and for computers you can download free programs like f.lux that you can customize for your child's schedule. These programs change the primary hue in the display, from white/blue to orange. White and blue light is stimulating, while orange light is relaxing. That's why shopping mall lights look very different from your bedroom, or at least they should!

3. Sleep Better by Eating Well

Just as your child's nutrition is critical throughout the day, it's equally crucial at night. It's your responsibility to monitor what your child eats for dinner and before bedtime.

Junk food, caffeine, and sweets cause a spike in the body's

stress hormone, cortisol, which puts the body under stress. That's why you initially feel awake and alert, but later when the sugar/cortisol crash comes, it leaves you exhausted and wanting more. Your child's body then spends time asleep working hard to digest and respond to junk food. A lighter, healthier dinner, on the other hand, allows their body to go quickly into deep rest. It's a good rule of thumb to give their body two to three hours to digest food between dinner and bedtime.

As a parent, monitor your child's reactions to certain foods and dyes. You may notice that red dye tends to increase your child's hyperactivity. As a result, you should avoid such dyes before bedtime (and other times as well).

And what about desserts? You can't complain when your child is bouncing off the walls if 30 minutes before bedtime you gave them a snack loaded with sugar. At that point, you've already lost the battle. It's unfair for you to demand that your child calm down. In some cases, they can't, even if you threaten punishment, which results in a lose-lose situation at bedtime for you and your child.

You need to be heavily involved in monitoring your child's sleep patterns. If you notice your child not sleeping, you need to address the issue immediately. Seek professional help if you cannot resolve the problem on your own, as there can be serious short- and long-term consequences of sleep deprivation.

4. Practice Mindfulness

Good sleep habits at night start with good mental rest habits during the day. ADHD children can get so focused that they obsess about their passions. This focus is great but can lead to burnout and exhaustion.

To avoid this, build opportunities for regular mental rest into your child's daily schedule. Mental rest means taking care of one's mind and giving it much-needed breaks. Encourage your child to be mindful of times when they feel mentally exhausted and to take breaks accordingly. Mindfulness is simply about slowing down the mind. It's excellent for pre-test anxiety or fearful social situations, but it is also beneficial in the daily routine. Mindfulness exercises may include focusing on a single subject that brings a sense of calm. It can be whatever works for your child. A simple option is to have your child focus on their breath, taking 10 slow breaths and then repeating. It's normal in any mindfulness exercise for their mind to wander. The challenge is to have them reposition their focus back on the intended goal, and over time this will build their ability to sustain attention in the moment. Another option is to have your child start a journal, maybe even a thankfulness journal, reflecting on the day and writing down several aspects of the day that caused them to be thankful. Journaling can be a powerful way to calm and focus one's mind, and the added discipline of cultivating gratitude has numerous benefits as well. There are many mindfulness techniques on the web that you can explore for your child (as well as for yourself).

Practicing mindfulness will help your child stay mentally rested throughout the day. It's also a great technique to use as a means of falling asleep.

SUMMARY

- Sleep is an essential aspect of the FastBraiin protocol for care.
- Lack of sleep may lead to significant impairment in a child's focus, mood, and overall health.
- Increase your child's quality of sleep by having a nightly routine that includes healthy eating, pre-bedtime rituals such as going to bed at the same time, limiting screen time three to four hours before bedtime, and utilizing mindfulness techniques.

CHAPTER 8

FLIPPING NUTRITION

How to Fuel the Brain for Increased Productivity

*"Don't be afraid to go out on a limb; that's
where the fruit is!"*

When it comes to fueling our cars, we don't hesitate to give them gasoline because we know that's what makes cars run well. We'd be foolish to pour any other substance in the tank, and we'd certainly pay for it later. But for some reason, when it comes to fueling our children, we don't consider the correlation between fuel and performance. We sacrifice their success by giving them sugary, processed, and dead foods instead of providing them with nutrient-rich, living, and empowering foods. A study published in 2010 in *The Journal of Attention Disorders* reported that the typical Western diet more than doubled the chances that an individual would be diagnosed with ADHD.[53] Although changing fuel sources may not remove the negative aspects of ADHD, the individual will undoubtedly be better off than they would be otherwise.

We must begin viewing food not just as fuel but as information that communicates directly to our children's DNA, impacting their entire nature, including their mood, behavior, and overall cognitive function. For your child to do their best mentally, physically, and developmentally, you must take their diet seriously. If a nutritional game plan is new or challenging for you, just remember, "Don't be afraid to go out on a limb; that's where the fruit is!"[54] Though we are not overbearingly strict in our approach to nutrition, there are certain principles to follow. To maximize implementation and sustain long-term success, we have purposefully kept our plan simple and straightforward. The following is an overview of our nutritional recommendations:

Decrease:
> Sugars
>
> Dyes
>
> Processed Foods

Increase:
> Vegetables and Fruits
>
> Healthy Proteins
>
> Healthy Fats

Use Supplements:
> Multivitamin
>
> Vitamin D3

Magnesium

Omega-3s

Phosphatidylserine

Let's take a closer look at each item in the FastBraiin nutritional game plan.

DECREASE SUGARS

People regularly ask our FastBraiin team for a list of foods that exacerbate symptoms of ADHD. At the top of our list are sugars and dyes. Sugar is well known to stimulate active and distracted behavior. Children with diets high in sugar may be four times as likely to exhibit ADHD symptoms than those who have low sugar consumption.[55] One of the big problems with sugar is the crash that occurs soon after it has been digested, causing a decrease in focus and an increase in impulsivity and frustration. How would you like to be the teacher at 9:00 a.m. in a classroom with 27 third graders after they've just eaten sugary cereal or syrupy pancakes for breakfast?

When we have a sugary drink or food, our glucose level elevates, insulin kicks in, and glucose gets pumped into our cells for immediate use or storage. The resulting outcome is low blood sugar.

Fig. 8.0

We initially get a surge of energy, but after just a few minutes, when the blood sugar level crashes, we feel sluggish, irritable, shaky, and hungry for more. The glycemic index indicates how fast sugar from a particular food enters the bloodstream. The higher the index number, the faster one's blood sugar rises.

You want to aim for low-glycemic foods that give your child a steady supply of sugar without the crash. For instance, grape juice is straight sugar, which will go immediately into their bloodstream. If, on the other hand, you give your child grapes, which contain fiber, the rate of sugar absorption will go down, and there is less likelihood for any crash. In this case, grape juice would be significantly higher on the scale than grapes.

The glycemic load, however, which is different from the glycemic index, looks at the total effect of all the foods served at the same time. When you mix foods higher on the glycemic index with those lower, you slow the absorption of the higher glycemic foods. Be mindful that consuming sugars on an empty stomach magnifies the adverse effect. You can reduce the harmful effects of sugar by pairing it with fiber, protein, healthy fats, and even a dash of cinnamon.

ADULTS AND CHILDREN HAVE STRONG EMOTIONAL CONNECTIONS TO SUGAR.

Protein smoothies are a good go-to snack, as they blend up the fiber in foods, and the fiber slows down the digestion and absorption rate of sugar. Smoothies are also a great way to successfully deliver fiber and nutrients from fruits and vegetables. Try adding more smoothies in your child's diet to increase fiber while still having something sweet and smooth to drink that isn't a sugary soda. For instance, you could try 4 ounces of plain yogurt, ½ cup of berries, 1 scoop of protein powder, 1 teaspoon cinnamon, and various vegetables like leftover spinach, cauliflower, or squash.

Sugar isn't as easy to spot as you might think. In fact, sugar has about 60 other names. These are sneaky and cheap ways used by manufacturers to increase sugar content and to do so without the consumer being aware. Some of the more popular names of sugar are high fructose corn syrup, sucrose, dextrose, and rice syrup.

Sugar hides in "healthy" foods as well. Beware of flavored yogurts, cereal bars, and fruit drinks. Children's needs vary, but typically, children do not need more than 3–6 teaspoons of sugar per day (12–25g). To put this in perspective, consider that a 12-ounce regular Coke contains 9.5 teaspoons of sugar, which is the equivalent of 39 grams.

If you read the labels of the foods you buy, you will see a long list of ingredients and probably find high fructose corn syrup listed as one of the primary ingredients. Whole grains are much healthier than white bread and white pasta. In addition to looking for sugar on the label, you need to look at total carbohydrates, as carbs turn immediately into sugar once digested. Bread, rice, pasta, and potatoes all contain a significant amount of sugar in the form of carbs. To find the real sugar content, subtract the fiber carbohydrates from the total carbohydrates.

Begin limiting sugars in drinks because that's where you are going to see the biggest difference and get the greatest reward for your efforts.[56] Then move on to snacks and desserts, and finally toward less sugar at meals. Your child may resist your attempt to implement changes to their sugar consumption because you are dealing directly with your child's reward center—the very same pathway utilized by addictive drugs, giving us a sense of pleasure. The dopamine receptors become worn out and the child needs more and more to feel okay, so they crave more and manifest common ADHD symptoms.[57]

Adults and children have strong emotional connections to sugar, but the good news is that the body will readily adapt to having less glucose in the bloodstream. You may first notice some withdrawal symptoms such as increased anxiety and frustration, but in just a few days their body will adjust and stabilize. Stay vigilant through the withdrawal period, and don't give in to your child's demands. Doing so will only start the cycle over.

DECREASE DYES

Dyes, especially red, yellow, and blue, have a strong correlation with behavior, mood, and energy levels. Working to eliminate food dyes from your child's diet can have a stabilizing and positive effect on their overall well-being. The colors in dyes make foods attractive to us, but when we consume them, they put more strain on the liver to detoxify them. They are found in many items in the grocery store and probably in your home. Read the food labels in your pantry and look for anything that says blue, yellow, or red. Due to the lack of FDA restrictions, they can even be called "natural colorings." Many candies have these colors. Food dyes are also in some salad dressings, meats, types of toothpaste, yogurts, vitamins, and many other items.

Try eliminating dyes from your child's diet for a week or two. Reintroduce them for a day and watch the effects on your child's emotions and energy level. It may not be immediate, but stay tuned. You will likely see unstable emotions, irritability, and hyperactivity. Figure 8.1 offers some helpful alternatives when trying to eliminate dyes.

INSTEAD OF:	CHOOSE:
Colorful Candy	Dark Chocolate
Doritos	Sun Chips or Oven Baked Chips
Colored Juices and Sports Drinks	Water or 100% Juice
Fruit Snacks	Fresh Fruit or Organic Fruit Snacks
Fruit Loops	Honey Nut Cheerios
Colorful Toothpaste	Tom's All-Natural Toothpaste
Colorful Ice Cream	Vanilla, Chocolate, Strawberry
Mountain Dew	Naturally Flavored Soda Water
Popsicles	Fudge Pops
Ritz Bits	Cheddar Goldfish Crackers

Fig. 8.1

If removing sugar and dyes isn't helping your child's behavior, or if you still see certain symptoms persisting, perhaps there is another food or additive sensitivity in their diet. Try eliminating one or more of the foods in Figure 8.1, or even the entire list. Researchers have linked several foods to issues with focus, attention, and hyperactivity, including sugar, processed meat (bologna and hot dogs), processed cheese, dairy/cow milk protein, gluten, and fried foods.

Try cutting one or all of these out for a few weeks, and see if you notice a difference in your FastBraiin child. If their behavior does not change, you may notice a significant difference when you reintroduce the food. It is vitally important to reintroduce each item only one at a time, two to three times a day for up to four days to see if there is a possible reaction. You may observe reactions such as increased anger, agitation, unexplained mood swings, brain fog, or various physical symptoms.

DECREASE PROCESSED FOODS

It boils down to the simple fact that if God didn't make it, it's probably not good for us. Most food companies tend to take natural ingredients and modify them, adding preservatives until the end product will last 20 years on the shelf. Foods made in laboratories and factories have little nutritional value when compared to foods sprouting in mineral-rich soil. Organic food is better for us, but not all food with the label "organic" is necessarily organic. It's important to look for the certified organic label to be sure. Groups such as the Environmental Work Group (EWG.org) are good resources for choosing the right foods at the best prices. Every year they publish the "Dirty Dozen," a list of 12 foods that are so contaminated they cannot be cleaned. They also publish the "Clean Fifteen," a list of 15 foods that are generally safe to eat even if not organic. In addition, they publish a guide, *Eating Healthy on a Budget*, for ideas on how to shop wisely.

INCREASE VEGETABLES AND FRUITS

Vegetables and fruits provide the body with essential vitamins and minerals. Without them, your child's overall health and cognitive ability cannot be optimal. Try to include vegetables and fruits as often as you can, aiming for nine servings a day. For young children, ideally try to serve ½ cup of four colors a day (M&M's don't count). For older children, serve them 1 cup of five colors daily, 25 different vegetables a week. The more variety of colors, the better. Be careful not to overcook your veggies because you destroy many of the life-giving nutrients in the process.

INCREASE HEALTHY PROTEINS

Protein significantly increases brain function, is essential for overall growth and development, lessens our sugar cravings, diminishes the cortisol roller coaster, promotes alertness, and facilitates feelings of well-being. Studies have demonstrated that protein and fiber help normalize glucose levels and prevent the rapid spike and drop in blood sugar from taking place. Because the body cannot store protein to use at a later time, it's wise to include some form of protein at every meal, and even at snack times. Protein is especially important at breakfast in order to prevent a morning crash that can throw off the entire day.

Protein also has a direct impact on your child's mood and ability to focus by providing the brain with amino acids. These amino acids become neurotransmitters, or chemical messengers, that influence cellular communication. When they are in high gear, your child feels more alert and positive and has a greater sense of mental clarity.

"Nutrition can really make a huge difference in the success of both adults and children with ADHD," says Dr. Sandy Newmark, founder of the Center for Pediatric Integrative Medicine in San Francisco and author of *ADHD Without Drugs: A Guide to*

Natural Care of Children with ADHD. "I've seen time and time again in my practice that simple nutritional changes, like adding protein to breakfast or lunch, can really, really make a difference."[58]

Don't be fooled into thinking food doesn't matter. A little protein can go a long way. Quality proteins are found in meats, fish, eggs, or nuts (nut butters are also an easy way to bring protein into the diet).

A simple formula for calculating a rough estimate of your child's protein requirements is to divide their weight in pounds in half, which gives you the number of grams of protein needed per day.

To help you think through how to achieve these protein requirements, here is a sample list of foods and their general protein content.

FOOD:	PROTEIN (G):
1 Egg	6
2 oz Mixed Nuts	6
2 Tbsp Peanut Butter	8
1 cup Milk	8
8 oz Yogurt	11
½ cup Cottage Cheese	14
1 cup Dry Beans	16
8 oz Greek Yogurt	23
3 oz Meat	18–24

Fig. 8.2

INCREASE HEALTHY FATS

Fat has gotten a bad rap over the last few decades, and unfortunately, very little of it is true. A new body of research has emerged focusing on the beneficial aspects of fat, and to everyone's surprise, fat is not the dreaded enemy that we thought it was. Healthy fats do not correlate with weight gain and heart disease. In fact, they have just the opposite effect.

FAT IS NOT THE DREADED ENEMY THAT WE THOUGHT IT WAS.

Fat has been shown to increase overall health and fitness. William Sears, MD, Associate Professor of Pediatrics at the University of California Irvine School of Medicine, uniformly states that "fats make up 60 percent of the brain and the nerves that run every system in the body. . . . The better the fat in the diet, the better the brain will function."[59] Vilifying fat has had tragic effects, pushing us toward processed foods, and because there is little flavor in processed foods naturally, food manufacturers have pumped them with the real enemy, sugar and artificial sweeteners. On top of consuming more sugar, many people today have a diet that is high in carbs, low in fat, and low in protein—the exact opposite of what many professionals now recommend.

We must, however, distinguish between good and bad fats. Healthy fats come from whole food sources like avocados, nuts, seeds, coconut oil, olive oil, fish, eggs, 2% milk, whole milk, and grass-fed butter. Bad fats come in the form of vegetable oils, margarine, and fried foods.

Good foods and good nutrients, especially healthy fats, fuel the brain to create more cells, which results in more connected and stronger pathways. The thicker the connected pathways, the better the brain works, recalls, stores, and remembers information. The net effect is greater clarity, focus, mood, and behavior. Healthy fats also provide your child with a sense of fullness, which helps to ward off hunger and prevent sugar cravings.

Some parents wonder which foods are best and at what time of the day. For the most part, it doesn't matter too much. As a general guideline, limit carbs for breakfast and lunch, eat snacks with protein, and eat dinner at least two to three hours before bedtime. Try keeping a journal of what foods your child is eating, when, and what positive and negative behaviors result.

Changing Out the Fuel: Jennifer's Story

One of my patients, Jennifer, was struggling with many issues, both at school and at home. She was depressed, overweight, unable to focus, and irritable. While meeting with Jennifer and her parents, it became apparent that her diet needed to change. We discussed the FastBraiin approach and changes that were required to replace the bad fuel with good fuel.

Over the next few months, we saw Jennifer become a new person, full of joy and happiness. She opened up about her past, sharing her binge eating when she was feeling down about herself or if her parents were upset with her. She would eat bags of chips and drink sodas while watching TV to cope or simply as a response to boredom, unaware of the bad habits she was developing.

According to Jennifer, the change in her diet was life changing! She describes the change here:

> My mother and I came to see Dr. Jim, and we learned about the FastBraiin approach and how important diet is.

When we went home that day, my mother got rid of all the junk food and soft drinks in our pantry. We changed our eating habits, and the results have been fantastic. It was a family change, too, not just something I had to change.

I lost 20 pounds through my new nutrition and exercise program. Losing weight has made me feel good about who I am, and I want to do better in school and at home. I appreciate my family's support helping me get where I am.

For Jennifer, we simply looked at her diet and what she was putting into her body and began replacing the bad fuel with good fuel. Optimizing her nutrition led to a host of beneficial effects that transformed every area of her life.

Managing FastBraiin with excellence must include a lifestyle of healthy eating habits, but unfortunately many essential nutrients, even in healthy diets, are lacking in appropriate amounts. Modern dietary habits, an increase in processed foods, and the reduction of soil quality have stripped our meals of important vitamins and minerals. The same foods that were eaten just 20 years ago provided us with significantly more nutrients than they do today. Supplements are an easy way to make up for our nutrient deficiency.

Others are turning to supplements as a reaction against medication or as a complement to medication, wanting to reduce dosages and side effects. The difference between supplements and medication is that supplements are not drugs—they are food. Supplements do not treat ADHD. They seek to give natural support to the body and brain, caring for the person as a unified whole and helping their brain to function and perform at an optimum level, which has the intended net effect of reducing ADHD symptoms. But not all supplements are created equal. The lack of FDA regulations, along with a rising market for supplements, has led some manufacturing companies to falsely advertise the ingredients in their products.

Because we at FastBraiin believe supplements may be necessary for ADHD care, and there is uncertainty and lack of regulation in the industry, we felt compelled to manufacture our own supplements and perform our own quality controls. We wanted to know without question what we are asking our FastBraiin children and adults to put into their bodies. With that goal in mind, we partnered with a top biochemist trained at Emory University, Dr. Gary Allred, PhD, and a top naturopathic physician, Dr. Matt West, ND, who has a large practice in Oregon. We are proud to provide our clients with an all-natural, safe, and effective line of supplements, knowing that each batch is tested for purity and immediately available for clinical feedback. If you don't purchase your supplements from FastBraiin, make sure you buy only from a respected and trustworthy source.

We recommend as a baseline supplement strategy that you give your child a multivitamin, vitamin D3, magnesium, omega-3s, and phosphatidylserine.

MULTIVITAMIN

The most important supplement we recommend for your child is a high-quality multivitamin. Important vitamins and minerals, and the necessary amounts of each, are responsible for a wide range of functions in the body, which include the immune response, growth and development, focus, and attention. As mentioned previously, in our modern diets we generally do not consume the recommended amount of vitamins and minerals. At the very minimum, we encourage you to give your child a high-quality multivitamin that includes needed B vitamins and folate. One study performed

with ADHD kids, ages 8 to 12, showed that
vitamin improved "emotional symptoms, c
pro-social behaviors" by almost 80%.[60]

VITAMIN D3

Secondly, we recommend that your child take vitamin D3. Multivitamins usually have vitamin D3 already in them, which can be great, or you can take them on their own if you need a higher dose. Vitamin D3 regulates over 200 genes and is involved in many important biological processes, including energy, growth, mood, immunity, and healthy bones and teeth.[61]

Although it's not directly tied to ADHD, it certainly influences mood and cognition, both of which can be troublesome for ADHD individuals. Deficiencies have been linked to type 1 diabetes, rickets, multiple sclerosis, and various autoimmune disorders.

The body naturally produces vitamin D through sunlight exposure, but with kids being indoors all day and covered by clothes or sunscreen when outdoors, this important vitamin does not get created as it should. A large percentage of kids who visit our office are vitamin D deficient. The Institute of Medicine recommends 600 IU of vitamin D3 a day with an upper limit of 2,500 IU for ages 1 to 3, 3,000 IU for ages 4 to 8, and 4,000 IU for ages 9 and above.[62] We monitor the vitamin D levels and adjust the dose based on the labs. The normal range is between 30–100 ng/ml, but the optimal range is between 50–70 ng/ml.

MAGNESIUM

Magnesium is a precursor to many critical biochemical reactions in the body. Deficiencies have been correlated with irritability and

attention spans. It has been reported to be the most defi-
nt mineral in the American diet. Anywhere from 50–75% of the
population could be lacking in optimum levels. Multiple studies
have shown that magnesium can significantly and directly reduce
ADHD symptoms. James Greenblatt, MD, author of *Finally
Focused: The Breakthrough Natural Treatment Plan for ADHD*,
refers to magnesium as the "miracle mineral," prescribing it as a
first-step natural solution to managing ADHD symptoms. "Magnesium is more than a promise," he says. "It is a much-needed
and effective treatment for the symptoms of ADHD, and a way to
eliminate side effects from ADHD medications."[63] For maximum
benefits, it is recommended to also supplement with vitamin B6,
which helps cells utilize magnesium effectively.[64]

In addition, most ADHD kids have trouble sleeping, and magnesium helps relax muscles and bring down tension, making it
possible to fall asleep and stay asleep. It doesn't force sleep like a
sleeping pill does but naturally rests the body to facilitate sleep.
In the world of FastBraiin, rest is huge for overall performance
and well-being. Magnesium can come in pill or powder form. We
recommend the following guidelines suggested by Greenblatt. For
adolescents (13 and older), give them 200 mg, twice daily; for
children 10 to 12, give them 100 mg, twice daily; for children 6 to
9, give them 50 mg, twice daily; for children under 6, give them 10
mg daily, in liquid form.[65]

OMEGA-3S (DHA AND EPA)

Other beneficial supplements for ADHD are omega-3 fatty acids
(DHA and EPA). You've probably heard of omega-3s for heart
health, but research is also showing their incredible impact on cognitive function, learning, and overall behavior. Omega-3s are now a
part of infant formulas for that reason. Studies show that individuals

with low levels of omega-3s perform worse on reading and working memory tests than those with healthy levels. Omega-3s are critical for neural growth, cerebral circulation, and optimum dopamine levels—all of which benefit ADHD children significantly.[66] Research suggests that the right amount of omega-3s may be close to 40% as effective as medication in reducing ADHD symptoms. When taking omega-3s, it's necessary that you give plenty of time for the supplement to begin impacting your child's behavior. One study found it took as long as six months for omega-3s to cause a significant difference in behavior and cognition.[67]

If you take omega-3s on their own, however, be aware that they have limited ability to cross the blood-brain barrier. To receive their full benefit, we want these healthy fats to make their way through the barrier so the brain can utilize them. This brings us to our next supplement, phosphatidylserine.

PHOSPHATIDYLSERINE

Phosphatidylserine (PS) is a phospholipid (fat) that's beneficial in its own right by increasing cellular energy and communication, protecting cell membranes, and fostering optimal usage of glucose in the brain. The net effect is "better attention, less impulsivity and restlessness, and better short-term memory."[68] PS also functions as a catalyzing agent to omega-3s, binding to it and carrying it across the blood-brain barrier. The brain can then utilize and benefit from omega-3s. Phosphatidylserine, therefore, should be a part of your strategy, and certainly if you are already taking omega-3s. These two supplements, omega-3s and PS, are a powerful combo. Beyond brain development and cognitive function, they may also specifically help prevent or reduce Alzheimer's disease as well as significantly increase the brain's ability to recover after a traumatic brain injury like a concussion.

TARGETING ADHD SYMPTOMS WITH SUPPLEMENT BLENDS

The first supplement strategy to help FastBraiin children is to cover their foundational vitamins, minerals, and omega-3s needed for overall health and brain function. With this baseline in place, we then recommend considering targeted supplements that are specifically designed to increase focus and learning while diminishing impulsivity. These types of supplements can and do work, and their implementation has been found to reduce or eliminate the need for medication. They can also be helpful as a substitute in the afternoon when children are coming off their medication, or utilized on the weekends to avoid medication tolerance from building up. There are several supplements on the market within this niche, but be cautious, as focus blends can contain unknown and undisclosed amounts of hidden substances. Also, beware of excessive levels of caffeine and stimulants, whether from synthetic or natural sources. In an unregulated industry, and with a desire to effectively care for our patients, we believed it was our obligation to develop a targeted supplement. Through careful research and clinical feedback, our team developed a supplement called "Focus A" as an effective, safe, and natural way of increasing focus while controlling for hyperactivity.

While there has been a swell in public interest toward holistic and functional care, the medical community has been slow to respond. Not long ago, at a National Academy of Pediatrics meeting, I got into a discussion with a fellow pediatrician. When she found out that I not only allowed but also recommended that my patients take supplements, she couldn't believe I would offer something that is not FDA approved. I asked her if she prescribed Vyvanse (an ADHD medication), to which she quickly replied that she did. I was delighted to tell her that I also prescribed Vyvanse and that my FastBraiin supplements worked almost 50% as well as Vyvanse, with little to no side effects. I then showed her the four pages of side effects in the Vyvanse pamphlet and asked her if she went over all of them with her patients. She walked off!

The point is not to criticize other pediatricians but rather to underscore that physicians are not taught about supplements in medical school or pediatric residency training. Too often we do not think for ourselves, but instead we take at face value the studies and brochures provided by pharmaceutical companies that suggest that medication is the only route. It's easy to see why this happens when you consider the billions of dollars wrapped up in pharmaceutical companies and the pressure they exert on physicians to buy and push their medication. I'm not against medication, which we'll examine in the next chapter, but I am against being pro-medication and anti-supplements. As a physician, this seems short-sighted and somewhat hypocritical. Our job is to care for children and adults, and that means we should use everything at our disposal to that end.

WE ALL NEED TO DO BETTER

After one of my grandsons was diagnosed at age three with type 1 diabetes, his parents had to clean out the pantry and completely change their diet overnight. While we all won't have to manage type 1 diabetes, we still need to do a better job with our food consumption. Billions of dollars are spent trying to tell us otherwise. We can't listen to those voices, nor can we listen to our internal cravings. The temptation is there, but we need to be strong and diligent and keep our focus on the big picture of healthy eating, which leads to better learning and happier kids.

Take a stand today. Go through your pantry and get rid of all unhealthy food. We need to take our fuel sources seriously: out with the bad and in with the good. The difference will be more than worth it. Optimization through nutrition will continue to benefit your child and your family. Should you fall back into unhealthy patterns, which is easy to do, don't give up. Recommit to healthy eating and get back on track.

Talk with your child's doctor about their nutrition. Ask the hard questions—does my child need a multivitamin, vitamin D3, magnesium, omega-3s, phosphatidylserine, or another type of supplement? Be proactive and provide your child with a healthy diet.

SUMMARY

- Treat food as fuel for your child's mood, cognitive functioning, and behavior.
- Decrease overall intake of sugars, dyes, and processed foods. Sugars hide in everyday foods like bread, flavored yogurt, and fruit drinks.
- Increase overall intake of healthy fats, vegetables, fruits, and protein.
- Limit carbohydrates, especially at breakfast and lunch.
- Eat protein at every meal and with every snack.
- Limit sugary snacks and desserts.
- Closely monitor the effects that certain foods have on your child and adjust as necessary.
- Supplementation is the only way to get specific nutrients into your child's body. Top priorities for supplementation include a multivitamin, vitamin D3, magnesium, omega-3s, and phosphatidylserine.
- Try a targeted focusing blend like Focus A to help control ADHD symptoms, reduce the dose of medication, or eliminate it all together.

CHAPTER 9

FLIPPING MEDICATION

How to Use Medication Effectively

"Medication must fit within a comprehensive strategy of care."

Any conversation in the ADHD world will eventually turn to the subject of medication. It's a polarizing issue for many, with some praising it as the fix-all option and others denouncing it as harmful and to be avoided at all costs. We at FastBraiin believe there is a middle path—one that neither glamorizes nor vilifies ADHD medication. We affirm that ADHD medication has both strengths and weaknesses and should only be utilized in an evidence-based manner within a comprehensive model of care.

The first time I meet with a patient, we explore multiple avenues, taking an in-depth look at their past and present, their home and school environments, their physiological and mental markers, as well as their overall nutrition and wellness. The goal is to get a comprehensive picture of the patient to see if medication is a necessary part of care.

Several factors may contribute to the patient's symptoms, and medication alone will not solve the puzzle. To start care with medication or to use medication as the sole means of treatment will inevitably leave important ADHD factors unaddressed. All too often, within minutes of seeing a professional, an individual is prescribed medication and sent out the door with no further help. Such a quick method of treatment cannot possibly address the complexity and uniqueness of an ADHD child.

Physicians prescribing medication in the ADHD world do not typically consider the overall health interaction. Medication was created to produce a desired effect in the patient, but most medications have a long list of side effects. Whoever is prescribing medicine does not usually review the child's lifestyle, nutrition, and other medication they may be taking.

The negative effect of quickly prescribing medication without a full assessment is that underlying issues are not addressed, comprehensive protocols are not established, and side effects may increase.

Medication can be a powerful tool when used in the right context, with the right game plan, and with proper professional supervision. Many of our ADHD children and adults know that without medication, they flounder and do not experience the success they desire. Parents and teachers alike can testify to significant benefits when their children are on medication.

Medication and ADHD

So how should we view ADHD medication? Let's begin with what medication is designed to do.

MEDICATION: IT'S ALL ABOUT REWARD

The major symptoms of FastBraiin are divided into three general areas:

- Inattentive (difficulty sustaining attention)
- Hyperactive
- Impulsive (inability to inhibit one's actions)

These three components manifest themselves in different ways in FastBraiin individuals, but at the root of all of them is the lack of perception of a reward or the misplacement of a reward in the wrong object. FastBraiin children are inattentive because teachers are boring (at least to them), and other things are more engaging. They are hyperactive and all over the place because they are super engaged with their world. They are impulsive because they perceive reward and quickly go after it. Medication, in general, seeks to alter these reward pathways, attempting to deliver rewards to the child so that they don't feel the need to go elsewhere to find it. Or as Dr. Ratey says, "Essentially, the brain won't do much unless the reward center is responsive."[69]

> ## WE SHOULD NEITHER GLAMORIZE NOR VILIFY ADHD MEDICATION.

There are two main classes of ADHD drugs: stimulants and non-stimulants. The most commonly prescribed drugs are in the stimulant class, which include amphetamines (Adderall, Vyvanse, etc.) and methylphenidates (Ritalin, Focalin, Concerta, etc.). Non-stimulants include drugs like Strattera (atomoxetine), Intuniv (guanfacine), and Kapvay (clonidine).

As we've discussed, nerves talk to one another by way of chemical messengers like dopamine and norepinephrine (both are critical for attention, reward, and the regulation of behavior). For communication to take place, the message must be sent and received across a tiny gap that exists between neurons. This communication, however, doesn't always happen. Even when one neuron is talking, the other isn't always listening.

When one nerve pumps out the messengers, some of these messengers cross the gap to the other side, and some of these messengers don't make it across and instead get reabsorbed back into the original neuron. When this happens, there is a communication breakdown, and that's where medication comes in. The goal of medication is to increase the levels of dopamine and norepinephrine in the brain, increasing the ability and likelihood that communication takes place between neurons.

Medication facilitates nerve communication by blocking the reabsorption from taking place. The amount of dopamine and norepinephrine that remain in the gap is therefore available to reach the other neuron. More neural communication translates into an overall increase in brain activity, learning potential, mood, and excitement.

It sounds counterintuitive that doctors would prescribe stimulants to overactive kids, but it makes sense when you consider that their hyperactivity is just their pursuit of reward and pleasure. Stimulation calms them down because stimulation is what they are already searching for—and with the medication providing the stimulation, the child does not need to go searching for it elsewhere.

Stimulants and non-stimulants attempt to alter similar pathways in the brain. Stimulants are faster acting with almost immediate results, while non-stimulants may take weeks and upwards of two months for the prefrontal cortex to respond appropriately. However, because non-stimulants don't actively increase norepinephrine and dopamine, they have no potential for abuse.

> # EVEN WITH INCREDIBLY DYNAMIC AND GIFTED TEACHERS, SOME KIDS STILL NEED MEDICATION TO HELP CREATE A SENSE OF RELEVANCE AND REWARD.

Medication is most commonly prescribed for issues of attention within the classroom. You've probably heard the words, "Your child just doesn't pay attention!" or something similar. These comments come from teachers who are trying to keep the class on task while your child is talking, doodling, or staring out the window. However, sustained attention is only as good as the stimulus—and in this case, as good as the teacher. Even with incredibly dynamic and gifted teachers, some kids still need medication to help create the sense of relevance and reward.

I experience this sort of thing myself. My attention is easily sustained when I'm watching the Clemson Tigers play football, but when I'm sitting in a meeting for an hour, and someone is going on and on through their 30+ PowerPoint slides, there's no chance at all that I'm paying attention. This happened at a conference on ADHD that I recently attended. I am convinced there were

5 of us with ADHD in this group of 200-plus, because all 5 of us had left the room and were hanging out in the lobby, unable to sit through the lecture any longer! Why? Regardless of our different reasons, we perceived something in the lobby as more valuable than listening to the presentation.

Our children's attention works the same way. I had one kid tell me, "My mind does not just wander, it leaves the building!" Sustained attention depends entirely upon the perception of reward. When the perception of reward takes place, motivation increases for that specific reward, and a sustained effort toward that reward becomes possible.

Fig. 9.0

Dopamine is a neurotransmitter associated with feeling good and is therefore heavily responsible for reward seeking. Whether it's through winning a video game or doing well on a math test, dopamine is at work. Motivation and the perception of reward go hand in hand. If ADHD children see no relevance and reward, even if it is a video game, they won't have any motivation to play. Medication seeks to directly influence this reward pathway, giving the child a perception of reward where they didn't previously perceive any value. That's why a child who finds a teacher boring can see that same teacher as interesting when on medication. And the same goes for any other activity. Math problems that were irrelevant become relevant to the child. Motivation and sustained attention increase as the child's perception of reward increases.

Let's think about your one-on-one conversations. How long do you have before the person you are talking to looks away? Studies have shown that the average initial attention span is 8 seconds. If you keep them interested, you will get 30 seconds, and then you might have a chance at 90 seconds. At 90 seconds, you most likely will lose everybody. If you watch their eyes as you talk, you can gauge their level of interest. If they are looking away, you've probably lost them. And what does that mean? I hate to tell you, but it means they've perceived something as more valuable than listening to you.

WITHOUT THE CORRECT INTERVENTION AND CARE, ADHD INDIVIDUALS WILL MOST LIKELY STRUGGLE.

We must also place the topic of sustained attention in the context of the environment. Our children's brains will naturally take their attention to the next most interesting thing around them— whether it's a text message, the pencil on the floor, or what they are going to do on the playground. That's one reason why teachers need to focus more on increasing engagement during activities rather than giving students more medication.

But the system is the system, and we must learn to work within the system to some extent. We likely aren't going to change the classroom or the teacher's style, at least not overnight. And though some schools are beginning to offer unconventional and creative approaches to learning that fit FastBraiin kids well, the majority do not. Though many FastBraiin individuals have found the ability to rise above the school system, the reality is that many individuals are not so fortunate. And in a similar way, the majority also continue to struggle as they enter the adult workplace, which generally continues to cater to the non-ADHD individual.

Even though the system is not conducive to learning for ADHD individuals, those individuals must still learn to operate within it. In the academic setting, grades, performance, and skill acquisition do matter. Even though we may disagree with the system, we can't deny its reality and turn a blind eye to it. That would be like assuming your fourth grader, who is performing poorly at school and has trouble listening at home, is going to grow up to be the next Justin Timberlake, Michael Phelps, or David Neeleman. They could, but there's no guarantee, and it's highly unlikely.

Without the correct intervention and care, ADHD individuals will most likely struggle. We affirm the strength of having FastBraiin, but as previously mentioned, constant battering to the ADHD individual's self-esteem and lack of understanding and guidance often cripple their innate strengths and leave them paralyzed.

There is certainly a need for our children to learn how to pay attention and control their impulsivity, even if it's within an education system we do not agree with. If we fail to address their lack of engagement and progress, we are setting them up for a host of possible negative outcomes—everything from lacking knowledge and problem-solving skills, to social and self-esteem issues, to potentially a lifetime of difficulty and struggle, including dropping out of school, incarceration, poor work performance, decreased satisfaction in life, and an increased chance of suicide. Parents should not take it lightly if their children are falling behind in school.

And this is where medication becomes a powerful option and counterbalance to the way our culture places unnecessary demands on FastBraiin children. By activating and engaging their reward pathways in the brain, medication can boost sustained attention, increase the likelihood that learning and skill acquisition will take place, and help protect against the litany of destructive patterns that can otherwise result.

With a little help from medication, the education system is less likely to bury the strengths of a FastBraiin child, and the classroom may instead become the playing field where your child's gifts and strengths can develop and shine.

THERE IS NOT A PERFECT PILL

Though medication can be an excellent tool for your FastBraiin child, it's not a tool that comes without risk. As you explore the value and possibility of giving your child medication, you need to be aware of the shortcomings of medication. Five weaknesses of medication include:

1. Medication Is Insufficient on Its Own

We've made this case throughout the book. Effective ADHD care demands a comprehensive and positive approach. A pill by itself does not help and could even do more harm than good. You can view medication like fertilizer. No farmer will mistake fertilizer for the crop or as the complete strategy, yet they know it is helpful as one component in the system, along with adequate water, sunlight, and cultivation. In the same way, one's medication must fit within a comprehensive strategy of care.

2.   Medication May Reinforce Poor Self-Esteem

The FastBraiin philosophy seeks to empower individuals with a positive sense of self. Medication runs the inherent risk of devaluing the person rather than increasing their worth. When a child takes a pill every morning so they can "function" properly like other kids, it can be hard for that child not to subtly internalize a negative stigma (they know other children don't take pills). There are several ways you as a parent can prevent the negative shadow of medication from being cast on your child. First, remember that your child is gifted; help them to understand their unique strengths. All conversation should be unashamedly positive. Second, talk about medication as a tool, not as something to fix a disease. Running shoes may help you run, but they do not make you a better runner! Third, make sure your child is never singled out in front of their peers or siblings because they need to take medication.

3.   Medication Has Side Effects

Short-term studies have demonstrated that stimulant medication, under proper guidance, is safe. There are, however, side effects to usage, as there are with any medication. If you look inside any ADHD medication pamphlet, you will see long lists of possible side effects. Most commonly, these include a decreased appetite, irritability, and dry mouth. Every medication and each level of dosage may produce a unique effect on your child. Therefore, work with your provider to find the right medicine and dosage. With deliberate effort and appropriate feedback, you will most likely be able to find a solution that works with minimal side effects.

It might be strange to imagine that increased focus could be a side effect, but for many FastBraiin individuals, it's something to consider. FastBraiin individuals tend to have incredible creativity, imagination, and relational abilities. Medications may decrease some of these natural gifts while addressing their weaknesses. The net result is that while on medication, your child becomes more like a worker bee and less like a Mozart. Many ADHD adults, for this reason, strategically pick and choose appropriate times to use medication—certain times require more linear and analytical thinking, like administrative or task-oriented work. These fit medication better than times that demand creative expression and spontaneous action, like brainstorming, meeting with a client, or in artistic and athletic activities. In those situations, you may find the absence of medication boosts performance. This gets to the heart of why we see the FastBraiin child as gifted. These are avenues that allow the child's natural giftedness to shine.

4. Medication Can Be Abused

ADHD stimulants are the most commonly abused drugs in colleges. Because these drugs target reward pathways in the brain, there is a possibility that chemical dependence and abuse may develop. The stimulants that are abused are the short-acting type that are crushed and even sniffed. For this reason, most drugs today come in long-acting formulations that extend the drug's activity, making them harder and less likely to be abused. Some stimulants, like Vyvanse, have a lysine molecule connected, which only allows for activation when the drug reaches the stomach. Even still, many people choose non-stimulants like Strattera, which have a low potential for abuse. It's important to remember, however, that psychological dependence is real and may take place with either type, stimulant or non-stimulant.

5. Medication Can Be Overused

Overmedicating, unfortunately, is a real concern, but doesn't have to occur if we rightly understand the place of medication in treatment and the reasons why we use it in the first place. Your child needs a qualified professional who is engaged and in tune with their behavior. Your provider should only use the minimum amount of medication necessary to facilitate the desired patient outcome. We advise a "start low, go slow" approach to determining a patient's dose.

It is also easy for adolescents and adults to begin requiring more and more medication to achieve the same results. An easy way to keep from building up a tolerance is to take a couple of days off each week. For most, this may mean taking the weekend off from stimulants. This break gives the brain an opportunity to rest and reset, which allows the same dosage to continue producing the desired outcome. We recommend that on your child's off days, they take a supplement. In that way, you can keep providing something that will help your child to curb and address their problematic behavior while still promoting brain health and preserving their stimulant response for the following week.

Many parents also find that supplements like FastBraiin's DHA, PS, and Focus A can decrease the dosage of stimulants needed, or they use it as an afternoon solution for when the medication wears off. In both cases, supplements can reduce the side effects and prevent tolerance from building up.

Medication Success

ADHD medications have been widely studied, and in general, researchers have found that more than 66% of children and adults who take ADHD medication benefit significantly. I have seen phenomenal results in my practice. During the past five years, we've collected data on thousands of patients. Over 92% of our patients have progressed from making C's, D's, and F's to A/B honor roll. Medication is not the full story when it comes to these children's success, but it certainly has played a role. If used correctly, medication can provide tremendous benefits, and the success of stimulants can be astounding. In most cases, grades go up, behavior improves, and overall self-esteem increases. These positive changes, which previously seemed out of reach, can become the new normal.

One story that stands out to me is Justin's. Notice in Figure 9.1 two pictures of Justin's writing, the first without medication and the second with stimulant medication one week later.

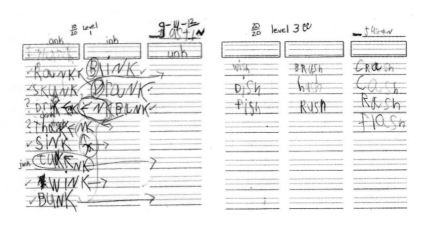

Fig. 9.1

What a difference! He went from making 10/20 to a perfect 20/20 score! How much better do you think Justin feels about himself now that he has a sense of accomplishment, his teacher can read his writing, and he's not embarrassed in front of his peers? And how might his sense of worth and confidence begin influencing other areas of his life? It's amazing to see the difference medication has made for his overall well-being!

Another story that stands out to me is Tripp's, who came to

see me as a struggling tenth grader. He was a D/F student. He was in trouble, and nothing seemed to work for him. After we placed him on medication, taught him how to learn, and encouraged him to believe in himself, he went on to make the A/B honor roll. The dramatic change surprised us all. What was most meaningful to me was how his outlook on life shifted from pessimism to embracing a bright horizon full of possibilities and opportunities.

Could Tripp have done that well without medication? Maybe, but maybe not. We'll never know. But without medication, the road forward would have been far more difficult and required significantly more resources, perseverance, guidance, and accountability. When I consider the gravity and difficulty of his personal situation, I think it is highly unlikely that Tripp could have achieved all that he did without the help of medication.

Should I Give Medication to My ADHD/ FastBraiin Child?

At some point, most parents ask the question, "Should I give medication to my ADHD/FastBraiin child?" Though medication is powerful, it does come with risks and potential side effects. The package inserts of most stimulants contain four pages of side effects and concerns. While success stories are great and medication can be a wonderful means of helping one focus and pay attention, I am constantly aware of and inquiring about side effects. Medication is helpful in most cases, yet I believe the less medication, the better.

I also believe in drug "holidays" that include all days when out of school and on weekends. However, I may utilize a lower dosage of medication on the days off from school, if the impulsivity, hyper behavior, and lack of attention are causing major issues within the family.

It's your job as the parent to carefully weigh the pros and cons of medication in the overall treatment plan for your child and to understand the side effects. You'll need to monitor potential side effects such as decreased appetite (leading to lack of weight gain), depression, anxiety, and migraine headaches. We recommend working closely with your health care provider to decide on a comprehensive plan of care. If your provider is using medication only, without an accompanying holistic plan of action, we recommend switching to a provider who will diagnose and treat the whole child, considering their various environments at home, school, and elsewhere.

Your child may do fine without medication, and you have the right to refuse medication if that's what you choose, but you should also know that refusing medication means the journey will require a lot more on your end, as well as from your child. If we take medication out of the equation, something else must fill the gap. That something else, be it extra time, structure, energy, and accountability, may be more than you or your child are capable of supplying.

Consider the spectrum of debilitation that ADHD is causing for your child. The more crushing and paralyzing, the more you should feel a sense of obligation and urgency to try medication with your provider's recommendation. Also, know that medication may only be necessary for a season. You don't need to feel like you are committing your child to a lifetime of medication.

If you decide to go the medication route, make sure you do not use it as a crutch, excusing yourself from the necessary work of addressing your child's learning and behavior issues. Medication may provide your child with increased attention, but it's your job to make sure they are focusing and headed in the right direction. Determine a comprehensive plan to address their symptoms, from nutrition to exercise to study techniques—and most importantly, don't let medication excuse you, as the parent, from your primary responsibility of loving and accepting your child just the way they are.

SUMMARY

- Medication is a powerful option in treating ADHD and should be considered from a balanced perspective of its strengths and weaknesses.
- The primary mechanism of medication takes place within the reward pathway of the brain. Medication allows for individuals to sense reward and pleasure when they previously did not sense any value, which has the net effect of increased focus, sustained attention, and reduced impulsivity.
- Treating ADHD involves more than simply prescribing a pill. Make sure medication fits within a comprehensive strategy of care rather than being the only form of treatment.
- The use of medication may reinforce poor self-worth, result in side effects and dependence, and leave important aspects of your child's ADHD unaddressed.
- If taking medication, it's essential to maintain a close relationship with your provider in follow-up visits to manage side effects, tweak the dosage, and evaluate outcome measures.
- It is important to promote physical health and prevent medication tolerance from building up by taking days off and using supplements.
- The degree of debilitation that your child faces should

influence the degree to which you are open to medication, if even for a season.

- It's essential that parents not let medication excuse them from their responsibility of loving and accepting their child just the way they are.

CHAPTER 10

FLIPPING THE PATH FORWARD

How to Stay Motivated
and Persevere

*"To get through the tough times, see
yourself, your child, and every conflict as
part of a larger story."*

We have covered a lot of territory about how to view, understand, and treat ADHD—from brain functionality and learning methods to exercise and rest to nutrition and medication—and
we've looked at impacting nearly every aspect of your child's life.
If you've read this far, I'm proud of you. It shows your level of

engagement, dedication, and desire. I hope it's been an informative read and, even better, one that will make a significant difference for you, your child, and your family.

As with reading any book, however, it's far easier to read and even agree with an approach than to implement and sustain that approach. Your zeal for change may be high after reading this book, and hopefully you've already started making some changes. But sooner or later that zeal is going to fade, and only a deep commitment will keep you going. With that in mind, in this last chapter, I want to leave you with a few closing thoughts to support you along the journey.

EMBRACE CONFLICT AND PERSEVERE

When was the last time you saw a great movie that didn't have any conflict? You probably never have. Conflict is the stuff of stories. It's what grips our hearts and keeps us wanting more. The best stories are the ones that have the greatest conflict and put the resolution in jeopardy—another girl's after the guy, the team is down with a minute left, or an important piece of evidence goes missing. The height of tension brings the climax, which prepares us for the powerful and beautiful resolution when they live happily ever after, the team wins, and justice reigns.

You and your child are in a story. Is there a conflict? Of course there is! And that's okay. It's okay to have struggle and difficulty. That's part of life and parenting.

To get through the tough times, you need to see yourself, your child, and every conflict as part of a larger story. Keep turning the page. Don't give up; the story is not over till it's over. I've seen so many parents that were in a place of despair and ready to give up, but through patience and perseverance, and the right strategies, they came out on the other side to a place they never thought was possible. If you can't see a bright horizon, that's okay. Keep hoping for a better tomorrow. Keep showing up. Keep loving your child and doing the best you can to lead, guide, and support them. I'm reminded of an encouraging poem along these lines, entitled "Keep Going":

When things go wrong, as they sometimes will,
When the road you're trudging seems all uphill,
When funds are low and the debts are high,
And you want to smile but you have to sigh,
When care is pressing you down a bit,
Rest if you must, but don't you quit.

Life is queer with its twists and turns,
As every one of us sometimes learns,
And many a failure turns about
When he might have won if he'd stuck it out.
Don't give up, though the pace seems slow—
You may succeed with another blow.

Often the goal is nearer than
It seems to a faint and faltering man,
Often the struggler has given up
When he might have captured the victor's cup,
And he learned too late, when the night slipped down,
How close he was to the golden crown.

Success is failure turned inside out—
The silver tint of the clouds of doubt,
And you never can tell how close you are,
It may be near when it seems afar;
So stick to the fight when you're hardest hit—
It's when things seem worst that you mustn't quit.[70]

EXPECT CHANGE AND ADAPT

The one thing you can count on with ADHD is that things will not stay the same. Everything is dynamic and always in motion and changing. We need to learn to adapt in real time to this ever-shifting world. Trying to implement the perfect plan (if such a thing even exists) is pointless because as soon as you do, your child will have entered a new stage of development—and a new plan will be needed. It's not that we don't pursue excellence; it's that we pursue a particular type of excellence—being willing and able to adapt to your child and their environment.

The most common challenge is adapting to your ever-changing child. Part of the FastBraiin philosophy is that we must meet children where they are, on their turf—a turf that changes daily, hourly, and minute by minute, which puts a degree of responsibility back on us as the parents and caregivers to continually be in flux with them. We must listen to our children, be in tune with them, be constantly learning from them to see how they are growing and changing so that we can correctly adapt our care for them in the present, not to the version of the child five weeks ago or two years ago. What worked with the 10-year-old needs to change to meet the needs of the 13-year-old in both communication and care.

You may have been doing great with your game plan, but if that game plan doesn't evolve with your child, it will be rendered ineffective. Our children are always changing, and we need to grow in our understanding and care of them. This includes knowing their passions, which can shift on a dime. You might find yourself going to basketball games and then to music concerts and then to the science museum. It may feel a little disorienting, but I challenge you to get used to the constant adjustment. Your child may surprise you with their next endeavor. Support them in whatever season they are in, and when they get interested in something else, let them go, and be there for them with your encouragement.

It is hard enough to manage an ever-changing child. We must also be cognizant of their ever-changing environments. It's far more important to be deeply in tune with your child than their environment, but the environment is still important. Primarily, this means staying in tune with their academic environment, where every new year brings with it new teachers, new classrooms, new curricula, new extracurricular activities, and new peers.

> # TRYING TO MAKE ONE ROUTINE WORK FOR EVERY SEASON OF LIFE IS NOT ONLY IMPRACTICAL BUT CAN BE COUNTERPRODUCTIVE.

Last year's protocol for studying might not work for the current year. The material may be unfamiliar, it might require more time, and the teacher may grade differently—all factors that will influence the routines you've set up at home.

School is not the only thing that changes from year to year. The home also has its unique changes. Different seasons of life put different demands on the family, not to mention siblings who also need to fit into the picture with their particular needs.

Trying to make one routine work for every season of life is not only impractical but can be counterproductive. Each situation calls for a different protocol. As your child's environment changes, be ready and willing to adapt to their needs with flexibility and love.

This also means being willing to adapt as research and applied science produce new ways of seeing and doing things. The primary responsibility to interpret and implement the findings will and should remain with your provider, but you still need to do your homework. You can't possibly learn all you need to learn from a patient visit. Your provider will also likely be coming from only one perspective, but as we've discussed, the ADHD/FastBraiin individual thrives within a comprehensive model.

It's important to remain open to how your provider or other professionals guide you based on recent research. Stay connected to those professionals who are cutting-edge and who are themselves evolving. FastBraiin is committed to being on the front lines, willing to change; we are not set in our ways. Every medical provider should have the willingness to accept a different point of view if the data points to an unexpected direction for the best possible patient outcomes. We talked about our child's mistakes as learning opportunities in chapter 3. The same is true for our parenting mistakes. They are learning moments, and these moments will never cease regardless of their age. I like how G.K. Chesterton once said, "a man who never makes mistakes never makes anything else."[71] Let's keep learning and see what happens!

CELEBRATE THE VICTORIES

Though your journey will have difficulties, expect moments that make it all worth it—the victories. What's important is that you not only notice them but also celebrate them. And victory doesn't always take the shape you want it to or occur in the way you thought it would.

Sometimes we as parents can put a label on success and project it way out into the future—getting into college, for example. Then we fail to notice all the "mini" victories along the way. These are critical to notice and celebrate, as they are opportunities to reinforce everything you are trying to teach your child. The positive emotions that you are building in those moments become the stepping stones your child will use to reach their long-term goals. Good behavior and good grades are not neutral; they are positive and should be valued and praised in that way. Progress by your child must be celebrated—for its own sake and as a means to encourage more progress. And be specific. Praise the particulars.

If your child makes their first B on a test, celebrate it. If your child diligently practices dance and performs well at their recital, celebrate it. If your child has a good attitude when you ask them to stop playing video games, then celebrate it. Big or small, whatever is positive that your child is doing or becoming, celebrate it. There's no limit to the joy you can express in these moments. Hug them, and tell them how proud you are, dance around the house, take them for ice cream—whatever it is that makes them feel special. You know their "love language" better than anyone, so speak that language and articulate it as well as you can.[72]

At some point in celebrating, make sure to have an intentional conversation with your child about where they are on their journey. Help your child see that success was possible. Reflect with them about the difficulties, pointing out their progress and diligence and how they achieved this moment of success. Since FastBraiin individuals have difficulty delaying gratification, connecting the dots between hard work and sacrifice toward a future goal is critical. Right as you say goodnight to your child is a wonderful opportunity to connect the dots for the day's celebrations and to say once more, "I love you and I'm so proud of you." These moments of reflection may teach important life lessons and become mental anchors for them to hold on to the next time they are in a valley or working hard to reach a goal.

FIND AN ADHD COMMUNITY

Any physicist will tell you that the hardest part about moving is getting moving, but once you do, momentum will help you keep going. Hopefully, you've begun implementing some of the strategies in this book and have broken through the initial difficulty of getting started. It would be nice if you could go on autopilot, but as with a car, you need ongoing maintenance. Cars need gas. They need oil changes. They need new tires. They may even break down from time to time. That's okay. It's part of the journey.

> # NO ONE DOES WELL ALONE.

One of the best means of providing ongoing maintenance and prevention, and to help with motivation, is to become part of an ADHD community for support. It could be an informal or formal community, but you need others who will walk alongside you. No one does well alone. We are social creatures, and we need each other. Develop your community, even if it's only a few parents with whom you can intentionally spend time together for mutual accountability, sharing, and encouragement. In an ideal situation, try to find someone who understands and shares your FastBraiin perspective on ADHD, who sees ADHD as a gift, and who is trying to implement a similar approach. My wife talks about the importance of her best friends and how they talked almost daily about their ADHD children and their struggles at home and at school. What they really were doing was supporting each other!

JOIN THE FASTBRAIIN REVOLUTION

Parents, I invite you to join the FastBraiin revolution. Embrace the extraordinary potential of your ADHD/FastBraiin child, and support them in their unique abilities. You have been given an opportunity to change the standard, and to change how our culture views these "active" individuals. Push, support, and help provide a pathway for your ADHD child while continually reminding them of their value and giftedness.

God didn't say "whoops" when He made us. We were each granted as human beings the same worth and dignity, each with unique differences and gifts. God created the FastBraiin individual to shine with energy, imagination, and the ability to turn speed into creative action—to be a difference maker in the world. If you take away anything from this book, take away the truth that your child is amazing—gifted, strong, passionate, creative, resilient, and brave. Believe it and believe in them. If you do, and you're willing to work with your child at home and school, everything else will fall into place. Allow your child to dream, allow them the freedom to be themselves, and allow yourself to dream alongside them!

It's my hope and prayer that you have found the content in this book valuable, that it will help you better love and care for your child, and that it will ultimately bear much fruit in your life and family. For further guidance, encouragement, and support, I invite you to visit us online at FastBraiin.com.

SUMMARY

- Caring for and believing in your ADHD child and supporting their unique FastBraiin strengths is a continual process that requires flexibility and adaptation.

- It's important to notice and celebrate large and small victories with your FastBraiin/ADHD child.
- We hope FastBraiin gives you hope and sparks interest and excitement as you consider joining the revolution to flip ADHD on its head.

APPENDIX

The Future of FastBraiin and ADHD Care

There are a lot of exciting things on the horizon concerning the world of ADHD. Things are changing and changing quickly. We at FastBraiin are privileged to be in the middle of the ADHD revolution that is sweeping the medical and educational landscape. The revolution consists of new thinking about ADHD, learning inside and outside the classroom, development and skill acquisition, parenting, and the importance of a child's self-esteem. FastBraiin is one voice among many who are beginning to question the system, and who are proposing bold and courageous new ways of thinking, understanding, and caring for the ADHD individual and family.

We live in an age of informational and technological advancement unprecedented in human history. We can hardly imagine life without smartphones and Google, but it was less than a decade ago that smartphones became a household item! The Internet has only been around for two decades. Since then, these tools, among others, have resulted in an explosion of information. More people connecting and sharing, and more people studying, researching, and inventing, with better and better tools, means growth is exponential—in all fields.

FastBraiin focuses on the ADHD individual, and because our method is comprehensive, advancements in many different areas have relevance and value. Our interest has been in the field of neuroscience, which is beginning to reveal to us an understanding of the brain that we never knew existed. The door in this world is just beginning to crack open.

Neuroscience has immediate application to the ADHD individual by offering detailed analysis and explanations of different types of brains and what is going on inside these brains, with an emphasis on the type of wiring—which informs the diagnostic side of ADHD. It's no surprise that ADHD has been significantly overdiagnosed. Yes, some teachers and providers have the knee-jerk reaction for medication, but there are also countless others who are genuinely trying to figure out whether or not a child has ADHD, and they are limited to what they can see and what they know. Making the correct diagnosis comes with a degree of subjectivity, but with modern advancements, researchers are laying the groundwork for future diagnostic systems, informed by current brain science, that will be far more accurate.

Beyond diagnostics, neuroscience is beginning to uncover exciting breakthroughs in cognition, learning, and the brain's connection to emotion. The connection currently found between our emotional center and the prefrontal cortex is opening an entirely new world in brain understanding. As research compounds in these areas, it's only a matter of time until they upend the traditional classroom and health care models.

Research and technology exhibit their relationship in other exciting frontiers, such as virtual and augmented reality. Some are calling augmented reality the next big thing since the Internet, which would, on that level, holistically shift our day-to-day experience. You may have heard of virtual reality (VR). In VR, you put on goggles and are immersed in another world. You may be less familiar with augmented reality (AR). In AR, instead of transporting you to another world, there is a computer signal that interacts in real time with your actual environment. You see the real world through your glasses, but overlaid on top of the physical world is a digital signal with various manifestations. Imagine seeing the Google Maps arrow on the road in front of you, or testing out virtual furniture in your room before you buy, or having fish swim around your room—VR and AR are limited only by one's imagination.

This technology isn't just for fun or navigation; it's coming to the education system and medical field in full force. VR and AR will soon have the ability to help diagnose, train, and teach in unprecedented ways. Companies such as Magic Leap are pouring resources into developing this type of technology at a tremendous rate. Instead of reading a book about Mount Everest, students can virtually go there, or to any place in time for that matter. Computerized skill-training takes on new avenues that are highly focused on skill acquisition and individualized toward learning strengths. Computers learn how you learn and adjust accordingly.

Programs are already in place to deal with a plethora of mental health issues, from brain trauma to Alzheimer's to—you guessed it—ADHD care. Virtual classrooms also open the potential for highly targeted tutoring and learning where FastBraiin students of all ages can learn at their own speed and according to their own strengths, being led through a review process until they master the material. With advances in assessment, training, and prevention, the impact of research and technology on the ADHD world will be massive, causing us to rethink the traditional ways we view education and health care.

The science of pharmacology is finally beginning to work with the neuroscience world, combining therapy with actual brain responses visualized through brain scans. These scans are now mapping brain connections to various stimuli as well as measuring and mapping responses to medication. This will, in effect, take a lot of the guesswork out of finding the right medication and dosage for each ADHD child and adult. To my delight, studies are increasingly focusing on co-existing conditions and emotional challenges to those with ADHD, including anxiety, depression, bipolar disorders, and emotional dysregulation.

New medications are always being explored. A brilliant psychiatrist and clinical researcher in our area, Richard Weisler, MD, shared with me information about an ADHD medication currently being developed that will last for 24 hours. If the side effects can be limited, this could be a real game changer. Newer medication seems to focus on minimizing side effects and increasing the longevity of the medication.

Not all is positive in the pharmaceutical business, however. Medication is less and less within the financial reach of the average consumer. As the price of medication goes up, it will be interesting to see how the market responds. ADHD supplements are becoming more popular, and there's no reason to expect this trend to stop. Because medication and supplements can be a part of effective care, it's on us as providers and health care professionals to continue doing our homework. We need to make sure that what we are asking children and adults to put in their bodies is safe and effective.

We've still got a lot of work to do to move forward, but the future of FastBraiin/ADHD children and adults is an exciting one. Our understanding of ADHD is growing every day. Better assessment and diagnostic models are being developed, along with highly targeted training and individualized learning protocols. And most importantly, there is a growing awareness that ADHD is seen as FastBraiin, not as a disorder. That, my friend, is very good! We are OKAY!

With many positive changes in the works and FastBraiin applying unrelenting pressure toward progress, I believe a future is coming when the medical and educational communities as well as individual families across the country, and even globally, will embrace the extraordinary strengths and potential of those with FastBraiin. I see a world where FastBraiin individuals are nurtured, accepted, and given a chance to let their gift of FastBraiin shine. I look forward to a world where FastBraiin and non-FastBraiin individuals learn to work together and mutually support each other's gifts for the greater good.

Let's get to work and make it happen—one person at a time.

NOTES

1. Hallowell, E. M., & Ratey, J. J. (2011). *Driven to Distraction: Recognizing and Coping with Attention Deficit Disorder from Childhood through Adulthood.* New York: Simon & Schuster, 52–57.

2. American Psychiatric Association. (2013). *Diagnostic and Statistical Manual of Mental Disorders* (5th ed.). Washington, DC, 61.

3. "Provisional Counts of Drug Overdose Deaths, as of 8/6/2017." National Center for Health Statistics. (2017, August 6). Retrieved October 11, 2017, from Center for Disease Control website: https://www.cdc.gov/nchs/data/health_policy/monthly-drug-overdose-death-estimates.pdf.

4. "Mental Health Surveillance among Children—United States, 2005–2011." (2013, May 17). Retrieved October 06, 2017, from https://www.cdc.gov/mmwr/preview/mmwrhtml/su6202a1.htm.

5. Inserro, Allison. (2018, January 14). "Psychologist Barkley Says Life Expectancy Slashed in Worst Cases for Those With ADHD." Retrieved Sept. 24, 2019, from https://www.ajmc.com/conferences/apsard-2018/psychologist-barkley-says-life-expectancy-slashed-in-worst-cases-for-those-with-adhd.

6. Dodson, M. W. (n.d.). "Feeling Separate and Unequal with ADHD." Retrieved October 06, 2017, from http://www.addgz4.com/slideshow/83/slide-2.html.

7. "Attention Deficit/Hyperactivity Disorder (ADHD)."Center for Disease Control and Prevention. (2017, September 05). Retrieved October 06, 2017, from https://www. cdc.gov/ncbddd/ADHD/data.html.

8. Hinshaw, S. P., & Scheffler, R. M. (2014). *The ADHD Explosion: Myths, Medication, Money, and Today's Push for Performance.* Oxford: Oxford University Press, 28.

9. A Conversation with Dr. Hallowell [Personal interview]. (2017, August 25).

10. The Hallowell Center. "Benefits (Yes, Benefits!) of Having ADD/ ADHD." May 2019. www.hallowellnyc.com/HallowellNYC/ LivingwithADD/BenefitsYesBenefitsofHavingADDA/index.cfm.

11. Archer, Dale. (2016). *The ADHD Advantage: What You Thought Was a Diagnosis May Be Your Greatest Strength*. New York: Avery Pub Group, 34.

12. Surman, C., Bilkey, T., & Weintraub, K. (2014). *Fast Minds: How to Thrive If You Have ADHD (or Think You Might)*. New York: Berkley Books, 143.

13. Hallowell, E. M., & Jensen, P. S. (2010). *Superparenting for ADD: An Innovative Approach to Raising Your Distracted Child*. New York: Ballantine Books, 5Wikipedia (2017, October 05).

14. "Hero." Retrieved October 06, 2017, from https://en.wikipedia.org/ wiki/Hero.

15. Dodson, William. (2017, August 04). "Secrets of ADHD Treatment." Retrieved October 06, 2017, from https://www.additudemag.com/ secrets-of-ADHD-treatmenttherapy-options-children-adults/.

16. Hallowell, E. M., & Jensen, P. S., (2010). *Superparenting for ADD: An Innovative Approach to Raising Your Distracted Child.*, New York: Ballantine Books, 5–6.

17. Roediger, H. L., McDaniel, M. A., & Brown, P. C. (2014). *Make It Stick: The Science of Successful Learning*. Cambridge, MA: Harvard University Press, 148–49.

18. Ibid.,151.

19. Ibid.

20. Ibid., 179–80.

21. Hallowell and Ratey, *Driven to Distraction*, 112.

22. Surman, Bilkey, and Weintraub, *Fast Minds*, 31.

23. Roediger, McDaniel, and Brown, *Make It Stick*, 23–45.

24. "World Records." http://iam-stats.com/records.php, accessed April 4, 2018.

25. Einstein, Albert. *Saturday Evening Press*. By George Sylvester Viereck. October 26, 1929.

26. Hallowell, E. M. (2011). *Shine: Using Brain Science to Get the Best from Your People*. Boston: Harvard Business School Press, 124.

27. Ito, J., & Howe, J. (2016). *Whiplash: How to Survive Our Faster Future*. New York, NY: Grand Central Publishing, 167.

28. Medina, J. (2009). *Brain Rules: 12 Principles for Surviving and Thriving at Work, Home, and School*. Seattle, WA: Pear Press, 5.

29. Ratey, J. J., & Hagerman, E. (2013). *Spark: The Revolutionary New Science of Exercise and the Brain*. New York: Little, Brown.

30. Scrudder, M., Hillman, C., et. al. (2016). "Tracking the Relationship between Children's Aerobic Fitness and Cognitive Control." Retrieved December 13, 2018 from https://www.ncbi.nlm.nih.gov/pmc/articles/PMC4993702/, accessed February 21, 2019.

31. H. van Praag et al. "Running Increases Cell Proliferation and Neurogenesis in the Adult Mouse Dentate Gyrus," *Nat Neurosci*, 2:266–70, 1999, as cited in Yeager, Ashley, "How Exercise Reprograms the Brain," https://www.the-scientist.com/features/this-is-your-brain-on-exercise-64934.

32. American Academy of Pediatrics. (2013, January 01). "The Crucial Role of Recess in School." Retrieved October 05, 2017, from http://pediatrics.aappublications.org/content/131/1/183.

33. Neck, C., Manz, C., & Houghton, J. (2006). *Self-Leadership: The Definitive Guide to Personal Excellence*. Los Angeles: Sage Publications, Inc., 133.

34. Chen, C. (2017). *Fitness Powered Brains: Optimize Your Productivity, Leadership and Performance*. London, U.K.: Brain & Life Publishing.

35. Ibid.

36. Ratey, J. J., & Hagerman, E. (2013). *Spark: The Revolutionary New Science of Exercise and the Brain*. New York: Little, Brown.

37. Ibid.

38. Ratey, John. "Exercise and the ADHD Brain," https://www.additudemag.com/exercise-and-the-ADHD-brain/, accessed March 21, 2018.

39. Iskander, Mona. (2011, February 8). "A Physical Education in Naperville." PBS. Retrieved October 05, 2017, from http://www.pbs.org/wnet/need-to-know/video/a-physical-education-in-naperville-ill/7134/.

40. Ibid.

41. Ratey and Hagerman, *Spark*.

42. Associated Press, "Exercise Found Effective Against Depression." *New York Times*, Oct. 10, 2000. Accessed March 8, 2019, https://www.nytimes.com/2000/10/10/health/exercise-found-effective-against-depression.html.

43. Ratey and Hagerman, *Spark*.

44. Ibid

45. Archer, Dale. (2016). *The ADHD Advantage: What You Thought Was a Diagnosis May Be Your Greatest Strength*. New York: Avery Pub Group, 50.

46. Medina, *Brain Rules: 12 Principles for Surviving and Thriving*, 14.

47. Reed, K., & Lawler, D. (2013, June 14). "Learning Readiness: Proven Interventions to Improve Student Wellness, Academic Performance, and Behavior." Retrieved October 6, 2017, from Readiness-Proven-Interventions-to-Improve-Student-WellnessAcademic-Performance-and-Behavior.pdf.

48. Campbell, Phil. (2017, August 25). "Sprint 8: Program Reduces Body Fat in 8 Weeks." Retrieved October 06, 2017, from http://www.sprint8.com/sprint-8-white-paper-summary/.

49. Jordan, Chris. "Make Every Minute Count with Johnson & Johnson's Official 7 Minute Workout App." https://www.jnj. com/health-and-wellness/make-every-minute-count-with-johnson-johnsons-official-7-minute-workout-app, accessed Aug. 2, 2018.

50. Joszt, Laura. "Possible Connections Between Sleep Issue and ADHD." AJMC. September 11, 2017. https://www.ajmc.com/newsroom/possible-connections-between-sleep-issues-and-adhd.

51. Wamsley, Erin J, PhD, and Stickgold, Robert, PhD. (2011). "Memory, Sleep and Dreaming: Experiencing Consolidation." *Sleep Medicine Clinics* 6, no.1.

52. "5 Big Benefits of a Short Power Nap." SACAP. February 13, 2018. https://www.sacap.edu.za/blog/psychology/power-nap/.

53. Research Australia. (2010, July 29). "Western Diet Link to ADHD, Australian Study Finds." ScienceDaily. Retrieved October 11, 2017 from www.sciencedaily.com/releases/2010/07/100729091454. htm.

54. Skully, Frank. Retrieved April 10, 2018. https://quoteinvestigator. com/2015/11/13/limb/.

55. Greenblatt, J., & Gottlieb, B. (2017). *Finally Focused: The Breakthrough Natural Treatment Plan for ADHD That Restores Attention, Minimizes Hyperactivity, and Helps Eliminate Drug Side Effects*. New York: Harmony Books, 124–5.

56. Ibid., 126.

57. Ibid., 125.

58. Additude Editors. (2017, April 18). "6 Essential (and Often Overlooked) Supplements for ADHD." Retrieved October 11, 2017, from https://www.additudemag.com/slideshows/ ADHD-supplements-fish-oil-zinc-iron/.

59. Sears, Bill. (2014, August 15). "Omega-3 and DHA as Brain Food." Ask Dr. Sears. Retrieved October 11, 2017, from https:// www.askdrsears.com/topics/feeding-eating/family-nutrition/ dha-and-omega-3s/dha-brain-food.

60. Greenblatt and Gottlieb, *Finally Focused: The Breakthrough Natural Treatment Plan for ADHD*, 31–32.

61. Naeem, Z. (2010, January). "Vitamin D Deficiency: An Ignored Epidemic." Retrieved October 10, 2017, from https://www.ncbi. nlm. nih.gov/pmc/articles/PMC3068797/.

62. Institute of Medicine. (2010, November). "Dietary Reference Intakes for Calcium and Vitamin D." Retrieved October 10, 2017, from http:// www.nationalacademies.org/hmd/~media/Files/Report%20Files/2010/ Dietary-Reference-Intakes-for-Calcium-and-Vitamin-D/Vitamin%20 D%20 and%20Calcium%202010%20Report%20Brief.pdf.

63. Greenblatt, and Gottlieb, *Finally Focused: The Breakthrough Natural Treatment Plan for ADHD*, 25.

64. Ibid., 23.

65. Ibid., 33.

66. Mercola, J. (n.d.). "Ultimate Guide to Omega-3 Benefits, Sources and Supplements." Retrieved October 10, 2017, from http://articles. mercola.com/omega-3.aspx.

67. Barragan E., et al. (2014, January 24)."Efficacy and Safety of Omega-3/6 Fatty Acids, Methylphenidate, and a Combined Treatment in Children with ADHD." *Journal of Attention Disorders*.

68. Greenblatt and Gottlieb, *Finally Focused: The Breakthrough Natural Treatment Plan for ADHD*, 116.

69. Ratey, J. J., & Hagerman, E. (2013). *Spark: The Revolutionary New Science of Exercise and the Brain*. New York: Little, Brown.

70. Guest, Edgar. "Keep Going," Retrieved March 20, 2018, from https:// quoteinvestigator.com/2017/04/21/do-not-quit.

71. Archer, Dale. (2016). *The ADHD Advantage: What You Thought Was a Diagnosis May Be Your Greatest Strength*. New York: Avery Pub Group, 34.

72. For more information, see *The 5 Love Languages of Children: The Secret to Loving Children Effectively*, by Gary Chapman and Ross Campbell (Chicago: Northfield, 1997).

INDEX

ABOUT THE AUTHOR

Jim Poole, MD, FAAP, clinical associate of Duke Health, founded FastBraiin in 2010 on the premise that individuals with ADHD have unique strengths in athletics, business, engineering, medicine, sales, the arts, and the classroom—wherever a quick and adaptable brain shines.

Dr. Jim's understanding of ADHD and the method of FastBraiin is the culmination of over 40 years of professional experience—listening to, learning from, and caring for ADHD children, youth, and adults. Dr. Jim graduated from Clemson University and the Medical University of South Carolina in Charleston, South Carolina, completed his pediatric residency at William Beaumont Army Medical Center in El Paso, Texas, served as Chief of Pediatrics at the Army hospital in Stuttgart, Germany, and founded his current practice, Growing Child Pediatrics in Raleigh, North Carolina. Today, Growing Child Pediatrics is an affiliate of Duke Health and one of the largest pediatric practices in North Carolina.

The philosophy of FastBraiin was planted early in Dr. Jim's life as he watched his father and fellow pediatrician, Dr. Frank Poole, care for patients and was taught to value each and every person, regardless of their background or socioeconomic status. This philosophy was also developed through countless experiences within his own marriage and family, practicing as a physician, playing sports, learning how to learn, reading and more reading, enjoying thoughtful and sometimes tearful conversations with patients, conversing with professionals who challenged and energized him, and overcoming and thriving with his own ADHD (and an auditory learning disability).

FastBraiin has helped over 5,000 children and adolescents move from C's, D's and F's to A/B honor roll, and helped more than 2,000 adults improve their productivity and relationships at home and in the workplace. FastBraiin currently has multiple locations within the Raleigh-Durham area with plans for a national expansion.

As founder of FastBraiin, Dr. Jim says: "I have a deep desire to help children, adolescents, families, and adults navigate the confusing and sometimes hopeless world of ADHD. For me, flipping my thoughts and understanding about ADHD has made ALL the difference—as a husband, father, physician, and friend. Those of us who are FastBraiin do not need to blend in with the rest of the world. We need to embrace our FastBraiin by developing our strengths, being grateful and excited about who we are, and sharing our gift with the world!"